1981

SYMBOLISM

An anthology

SYMBOLISM
An anthology

Edited and translated by
T.G. West

METHUEN
London & New York

First published in 1980 by
Methuen & Co. Ltd
11 New Fetter Lane, London EC4P 4EE
Published in the USA by
Methuen & Co.
in association with Methuen, Inc.
733 Third Avenue, New York, NY 10017
© 1980 T.G. West
Printed in Great Britain by
J.W. Arrowsmith

British Library Cataloguing in Publication Data

Symbolism
    1. Literature, Modern–19th century – History and criticism –
    Addresses, essays, lectures
    2. Literature, Modern–20th century – History and criticism –
    Addresses, essays, lectures
    3. Symbolism in literature – Addresses, essays, lectures
    I. West, Thomas G
809'.03'4.   PN760.5   80-40894

ISBN 0-416-71890-6
ISBN 0-416-71900-7 Pbk

Contents

Acknowledgements

The editor and publishers wish to record their thanks for permission to use copyright material by W. B. Yeats, Paul Valéry and Wallace Stevens: to Mrs W. B. Yeats, Macmillan London Limited and Macmillan Publishing Co., Inc., New York, for 'The Symbolism of Poetry' and 'A General Introduction for my Work' © Mrs W. B. Yeats, 1961; to Routledge and Kegan Paul Ltd, London, and Princeton University Press, for 'Remarks on Poetry'; to Faber and Faber Ltd, London, and Alfred A. Knopf Inc., New York, for 'Imagination as Value'.

The sources of the texts used in this anthology are as follows: 'Crise de vers' by Stéphane Mallarmé in *Œuvres complètes*, ed. Mondor and Jean-Aubry (Paris, 1945). 'The Symbolism of Poetry' and 'A General Introduction for my Work' by W. B. Yeats in *Essays and Introductions* (London, 1961). 'Propos sur la poésie' by Paul Valéry in Volume I of the *Œuvres complètes*, ed. Hytier (Paris, 1957). 'Poesie und Leben' and 'Drei kleine Betrachtungen' by Hugo von Hofmannsthal in *Prosa I* and *Prosa IV* of the *Gesammelte Werke*, ed. Steiner (Stockholm, 1953–64). 'Auguste Rodin: Zweiter Teil' (extract) and 'Der Brief des jungen Arbeiters' by R. M. Rilke in Volumes V and VI of the *Sämtliche Werke*, ed. Zinn (Frankfurt, 1955–66). 'Imagination as Value' by Wallace Stevens from *The Necessary Angel: Essays on Reality and the Imagination* (London, 1960). 'Magiya slov' by Andrei Bely in *Simvolizm* (Moscow, 1910). 'O sovremennom sostoyanii russkogo simvolizma' by Aleksandr Blok in Volume V of the *Sobranie sochinenij v vos'mi tomax*, ed. Orlov *inter alios* (Moscow-Leningrad, 1960–3).

Introductory note

In bringing together essays by eight writers associated with symbolism in literature, this anthology aims to provide readers of English with material to complement the study of one or more national literatures during the period of symbolist activity. The selection has been determined above all by a concern for the quality and enduring importance of the writer's literary production – thus Wallace Stevens, R. M. Rilke and Paul Valéry, though less closely linked to a symbolist school, have been preferred to such influential figures as Paul Verlaine, Jean Moréas, Stefan George and Valery Bryusov. Such preference implies a broad definition of the symbolist movement and its principles. In choosing authors and texts my desire was not, however, to promote or challenge a definition but to make available representative essays of writers whose works will figure prominently in surveys and in theories of symbolism. There are regrets for not including more writers and literatures but I felt letting a small number have a good say would be more useful than letting a large number speak in telegraph style. The essays by the Russian writers Andrei Bely and Aleksandr Blok appear in English for the first time and it is hoped they will assist the growing appreciation of their works in the West.

The origin and realization of this anthology are greatly indebted to Professor Lilian R. Furst and I take pleasure in acknowledging to her my thanks and gratitude. I am grateful to my colleague Dr John Elsworth for his criticism and careful reading of my translation of Andrei Bely's article. To my friend Françoise Bernard who oversaw the whole work and brought to light many a difficult phrase I dedicate this book with thanks and affection.

THOMAS WEST
Norwich, Autumn 1979

Stéphane Mallarmé

Stéphane Mallarmé (1842-98) was born in Paris to a family associated for generations with the civil service. He grew up in the provinces under the care of his grandmother after his mother's death when he was four. The death of his only sister ten years later affected him deeply. By becoming an English teacher, he escaped the family tradition. In 1863 he married the German girl, Marie Gerhard. There followed a series of desolate assignments in Tournon, Besançon and Avignon. After 1871 he lived in Paris and from 1875 at 87 rue de Rome, the gathering-spot on Tuesday evenings for a legion of tiros, among them, Paul Claudel, André Gide, Stefan George, Georges Rodenbach, Paul Valéry and Arthur Symons.

WRITINGS

As potent as they are rare: *L'Après-midi d'un Faune* (*The Afternoon of a Faun*, 1876; written 1865); a textbook, *les Mots anglais; Poésies* (1887; poetry since 1862); translations and a collection of criticism *Divigations* (1897); other important fiction was collected posthumously.

'Crisis in Verse' draws on material written between 1886 and 1896 and appeared complete in *Divigations*.

CRISIS IN VERSE

Overtaken just now by the weariness brought on by miserable weather one afternoon after the next, in a languorous gesture I let the fringe of colourful glass beads fall across the window; and with no curiosity, save that of having read them all twenty years ago, I gaze at the bindings in the bookcase whose glimmer is aligned with a new light: and so now I shall attempt to follow the lights of the present storm through the mellow sky, peering at the window while I write.

If it is not ending, a recent phase of poetry has paused or perhaps has become conscious of itself: an unusual curiosity about poetry elicits new creativity and relative confidence.

Even the press, usually twenty years behind events, suddenly deals with the subject punctually.

Literature is now experiencing an exquisite and fundamental crisis.

Whoever grants literature a primary importance – or any importance – must recognize the momentousness of the present hour: we are witnessing upheavals which suggest the finale of a century, not, however, like those of the last; now, by contrast, outside the public arena, we are watching a disturbance of the temple's veil, meaningful folds and, to a certain extent, its rending.

A French reader, whose habits were interrupted by the death of Victor Hugo,[1] can only be disconcerted. In the course of his mysterious mission, Hugo reduced all prose – philosophy, eloquence, history – to verse, and as he incarnated verse itself he virtually confiscated the thinker's, the orator's and the historian's right to expression: a monument in a silent desert, he was as well the concealed god of a majestic, unconscious idea which said that the form we call verse is itself, quite simply, literature; and furthermore that verse exists as soon as there is emphatic diction, and rhythm, as soon as there is style. Poetry waited respectfully, so to speak, for the giant – who identified it with his increasingly firm and tenacious blacksmith's hand – to disappear; and then it broke loose. The entire language had been geared to prosody and drew from it the vital sense of pause; but then it broke away, scattering freely its innumerable basic elements, having suddenly become like a verbal orchestration of multiple sounds.

Verlaine, in his fluid verse, secretly and unexpectedly prepared this development in poetry by returning to the primitive elements of language.

I followed with undivided attention this adventure in which I was supposed to have had a role more decisive than anyone can have. Now it is time to speak of it, preferably at a distance, anonymously, as it were.

It must be agreed that French poetry, because of the primacy attached to rhyme's ability to enchant, shows itself to be intermittent throughout its evolution. It sparkles for a while, dies down, then waits; it disappears altogether or perhaps wears away to the naked thread; there is repetition. Yet now, the century-long period of orgiastic excess, comparable only to the Renaissance, in no way passes into the chill and shadow of a new period – not at all! – rather, the poetic urge continues with renewed, though different, sparkle, responding to new circumstances. Moreover, poetic revival, once an imperceptible affair, is taking place publicly now as poets openly indulge in delightful approximations.

One can distinguish, I think, three attitudes towards the handling of the hieratic canon of the line of verse, varying from qualified reverence to outright rejection.

Its rules being so few, traditional prosody is virtually intractable – it sanctions the wisdom of certain activities, the use of the hemistich, for example, and turns against the slightest attempt to simulate versification like a law which views abstinence from theft as an exemplary state of uprightness. But this is precisely what matters little to learn, for if one has not understood it alone from the start, it is useless to submit to it.

Those who have remained faithful to the alexandrine, our hexameter, have loosened internally its rigid and childish metrical mechanism; freed from its overbearing rhythmic formulas, the ear now delights foremostly in perceiving the full range of possible combinations and relations of twelve sounds.

Here is an example of what is modern in today's poetry.

That poet with a sharp touch who still reckons the alexandrine to be the ultimate jewel, though one to be displayed like a
sword or a flower, rarely and for a carefully considered end,
handles it with reverence; or pretending to use it – almost
drawing out its finest sounds before delivering up the real thing,
splendid and naked – he allows his fingering to falter on the
eleventh syllable or to carry on to a thirteenth: M. Henri de
Régnier[2] excels in these accompaniments which display both
the discreet and proud inventiveness of a singular mind and the
temporary anxiety of all performers before the age-old instrument. Another attitude, or perhaps just the opposite one, is
reflected in that purposeful rejection of the old, tired-out mould
– for example by Jules Laforgue[3] who first introduced us to the
undeniable charm of lines without the correct number of syll-
ables.

Until now, as made clear by these two examples, there has
been little else than reserve on the one hand and exaggeration on
the other, due to the fatigue brought on by an abuse of the
national rhythm whose display, like that of the flag, must
remain exceptional. At the same time, however, there has been
an important development in our sense of delicacy, which now
admits deliberate metrical infractions and the fine dissonances
they produce. And only fifteen years ago – pedants that we were
– we would have felt annoyed by what seemed to be an illiterate
sacrilege! But it should be said that the strict line of verse, the
alexandrine, haunts and exerts a beneficial influence upon the
present experiments.

The novelty of free verse in our day (unlike that in the fables
and operas of the seventeenth century which was only a loose,
non-stanzaic arrangement of various well-known metres)
derives entirely from what should be called its 'polymorphic'
nature; now we are witnessing all degrees of disintegration of the
official line of verse, and applaud it as long as it gives us the old
pleasure. For example, M. Moréas's[4] recent verse – frag-
mented, with a delightful and ingenious precision – whose

euphony the reader instinctively agrees to perceive; or M. Vielé-Griffin's[5] gesture which scans – languid with reverie, startled with passion; and, prior to these, M. Kahn's[6] expert notation of the tonal value of words. These are only some of the names – others would serve as well: MM. Charles Morice,[7] Verhaeren,[8] Dujardin,[9] Mockel[10] – consult their works; they confirm what I have said.

The remarkable thing is that, for the first time in the literary history of any country, along with the general and traditional grand organs on whose freely accessible keyboard the orthodoxy is exalted, anyone with an individual technique and ear can build his own instrument once he is able skilfully to blow, pluck or strike it; it can be played along with others and dedicated to Language.

In this way a great freedom has been recently acquired; and my firm belief is that, with this new freedom, no beauty of the past has been destroyed. I am convinced that our solemn traditions, whose preponderance attests to the classical genius, will always be observed: and when it is inappropriate to disturb the venerable echoes, for sentimental or narrative purposes, we shall try to avoid doing so. But a soul exists only when its melody is played, and to this end everyone has his own flute or viol.

In my opinion the true condition and possibility not only for self-expression but also for free personal inflexion have been late in coming.

Languages being imperfect because they are so numerous, the supreme one is missing: since thought is writing without accessories or whispering without uttering the immortal Word, the diversity of idioms on the earth prevents anyone from producing words which would bear the direct imprint of Truth incarnate. This is nature's own proscription (we resign ourselves to it with a smile); and so we have no reason to consider ourselves God. However, when I turn my mind to aesthetics, I must regret that language cannot express things by means of striking keys which correspond to the colour and movement of the instrument of the voice as it can be used in several languages or sometimes only in one. In comparison to the word *ombre* which is opaque, the word *ténèbres* is not very dark; and how disconcerting is the perverseness which lends, contradictorily, dark tones to the sound *jour* and bright ones to the sound *nuit*! We want words with both a luminous (or dark) sound and meaning: yet if we had these, let us not forget, *verse would not exist*: the purpose of verse, as a complement to language, is to redress its shortcomings with wisdom.

This is strange; and it is equally strange – and consequential – that prosody's origins lie in pre-conscious times.

Would only a middling expanse of words on a page take on a definitive form beneath a comprehending glance, followed by silence!

For the French, the inventiveness of the individual need not challenge prosodic convention, although indignation would erupt if a singer who had left the well-worn path and strolled at his pleasure should be unable, in the midst of an infinity of little flowers along the new path, to gather them up and sing them as though before a conventional score. Recently such an attempt has been made, and research continues into, for example, the nature of accentuation, etc. At the same time many poets continue to play with recognizable fragments of the old line, looking back at it or away from it – as opposed to searching for an entirely new and surprising form. Constraints removed, a new school was able to make valuable experiments, but the zeal should now be contained, for the freedom it has glorified – that each individual brings with him a prosody as distinctive as his own breathing (along with the right to idiosyncratic orthography) – has encouraged no small measure of buffoonery and provided prefacers with a platform. Lines of verse will be similar because they will be regular and the old proportions will prevail, because the poetic act consists in perceiving quickly that an idea can be divided into a number of equally valuable motifs which must be ordered. They rhyme – and this provides the stress for, or the external seal upon, the metre they share.

The crisis in poetry lies less with that fascinating interregnum or pause in prosodic activity than with changes in our basic mental disposition.

For now we unquestionably hear sunshine as rays of light penetrate the meanderings of gilded melody: for Music since Wagner[11] has combined with Verse to form Poetry.

Either of these two elements may be developed integrally and triumphantly apart, not as a spoken poem but as a muted concert of its own; or the poem can be invigorated by their community, as instrumentation gleams even behind the veil of orchestration, and words lose their meaning in the darkened realm of sound. Whether willed or not by the musician, the meteor of modern times, the symphony, approaches thought which is itself no longer limited to expression in an everyday language.

And so Mystery explodes in the heavens of its impersonal magnificence where the orchestra seems fated to influence that ancient effort to translate it into language alone.

A sign which thus points at two complementary activities.

The Decadent or Mystic Schools, as they call themselves – or were hastily labelled by our newspapers – converge in an idealism which, like a fugue or a sonata, shuns natural materials, seems to be hostile to any thought which orders them precisely, and preserves only the suggestiveness of things. The goal is to establish a precise relationship between two images and to draw out from them a third quality which the imagination easily grasps and assimilates. We must abandon that aesthetic error – though it has informed many a masterpiece – which insists that the poem must portray the dense, intense wood of the trees rather than the horror of the forest or the silent thunder scattered amongst the leaves. Some pure self-expression, trumpeted heavenwards with skill, awakes a palatial form – the only inhabitable one – on whose absent stones the book closes perfectly.

Description conceals the fullness and intrinsic virtues of monuments, the sea and the human face; evocation, *allusion* or *suggestion*, though somewhat casual terms, point to what may be a very decisive trend in literature, one which both limits and sets free; for the special charm of the art lies not in the handful of dust, so to speak, not in the containing of any reality through description, in a book or a text, but in freeing from it the spirit, that volatile dispersion which is the musicality of nothing.*

Speech has only a commercial interest in the reality of things. In literature, allusion is enough; the essence is distilled and embodied in some idea.

And song, when it becomes a joy freed of material constraint, arises in the same manner.

I call this goal Transposition – Structure is a different one.

The pure work implies the disappearance of the poet-speaker who yields the initiative to words animated by the inequality revealed in their collision with one another; they illuminate one another and pass like a trail of fire over precious stones, replacing the audible breathing of earlier lyrical verse or the exalted personality which directed the phrase.

The structure of a book of verse must arise throughout from internal necessity – in this way both chance and the author will be excluded; a subject will imply inevitably the harmony of the parts brought together and, since every sound has an echo, their corresponding locations in the volume. Thus similarly constructed motifs will move in space till there is equilibrium. There will be neither the sublime incoherence of the Romantic page-settings nor the artificial unity imposed upon the book by a compositor's calculations: everything will be fluid, the arrangement of parts, their alternation and interruption by blank spaces, and will yield a total rhythmic movement, the

* Extract from *Music and Letters*.[12]

silent poem itself, translated in its own way by each unit of the structure. The instinct for such a work seems to be hinted at in a number of recent publications where some young poets seem disposed towards a goal similar and complementary to our own. They stress the perfect and stunning structure of a poem and mumble about the magic concept of the ultimate Work. Likewise some symmetry, which will arise from the relation of lines within the poem and poems within the volume, will reach out beyond the volume to other poets who will themselves inscribe on spiritual space the expanding paraph of genius, anonymous and perfect like a work of art.

Thought alone of a chimera reveals – by the reflection from its scales – how much the present phase of poetry, the last quarter of the century, owes to some absolute flash of lightning. The ensuing downpour has washed away the indeterminate rivulets of the older poetry from my window panes and brought forth a new light, revealing that virtually all books contain versions of certain well-known themes and that there might be only one book on earth, the Bible of all the world's bibles; and the only difference between the various works might merely be the interpretations proposed by all those ages we call civilized or literary for the one authentic text.

Certainly I never sit in the tiers of a concert hall without perceiving, in the sublime darkness, some primitive version of a poem which dwells deep in human nature, and which can be understood because the composer knows that in order to convey its vast contour he must resist the temptation to explain. And so I imagine, no doubt heeding a writer's ineradicable instinct, that nothing endures if it is not uttered; and since the great rhythms of literature are being broken down, as I have said, and dispersed in fragmentary rhythmic units or orchestrated vocables, we need just now to investigate the art of transposing the symphony to the book: this would be nothing more than a realization of our own wealth. For Music must undeniably result from the full power of the intellectual word, not from the elemental sounds of strings, brass and woodwind: it must be a full, manifest totality of relationships.

One of the undeniable desires of my age is to separate the functions of words, with the result that there is a crude and immediate language on the one hand and an essential language on the other.

The former use of language in narration, instruction and description – necessary of course, though one could get by with a silent language of coins – is reflected by the ubiquitous *journalism* which attracts all forms of contemporary writing except literature.

What purpose, ask those who use the latter language, is served by the miracle which transposes a natural phenomenon into a disappearing aural one by the device of written language – if it is not to allow the pure idea to arise from it, divorced of its direct and material associations?

And so when I make the sound – a flower – out of the oblivion to which my voice relegates all contours, something other than the visible petals arises musically, the fragrant idea itself, the absent flower of all bouquets.

Whereas, in the hands of the mob, language functions as a collection of meaningful coins, in those of the Poet it reaches its full potential, as an art dedicated to fiction, above all in dream and in song.

With several words the line of verse constructs a completely new word, foreign to the language and a part, it seems, of an incantation; and thus it perfects the separation of the word: denying, in a sovereign gesture, any chance – any descriptive sense which may have lingered in spite of the artful renewal both in meaning and sonority; and so you feel the surprise of never having heard any such fragment of speech, whilst, at the same time, your recollection of the object named bathes in a new atmosphere.

Notes

1 Victor Hugo (1802–85).

2 Henri de Régnier (1864–1936) began using *vers libre* in *Poèmes anciens et romanesques* (1890), returning to more traditional prosody in *Tel qu'en songe* (1892) and poems collected in *Les Jeux rustiques et divins* (1897).

3 Jules Laforgue (1860–87) made his poetry out of neologisms, free verse and popular rhythms in *Les Complaintes* (1885) and *L'Imitation de Notre-Dame la Lune* (1886).

4 Jean Moréas, pseudonym of Jean Papadiamantopoulos (1856–1910), the founder of the symbolist school with his manifesto of 1886. He published two collections of poems, *Le Pèlerin passionné* (1890) and *Sylves* (1893).

5 Francis Vielé-Griffin (1863–1937) expounded the theory of *vers libre* in *Les Entretiens politiques et littéraires* (1890–2).

6 Gustave Kahn (1859–1936), co-founder with Moréas and P. Adam of important symbolist-oriented reviews of the 1880s and 1890s, *La Vogue* and *Le Symboliste*. His thoughts on versification appear in the preface to *Palais nomades* (1887); other collections of poetry are *Chansons d'amant* (1891) and *La Pluie et le Beau Temps* (1895).

7 Charles Morice (1861–1919), publicist of the symbolist cause in *Demain: Question d'esthétique* (1888), later called *La Littérature de tout à l'heure*. He wrote a play, *Chérubim* (1891).

8 Émile Verhaeren (1855–1916), a Belgian of French expression, was a poet of the modern world, using irregular lines and speech-like rhythms; he published *Campagnes hallucinées* (1893) and *Villes tentaculaires* (1895).

9 Édouard Dujardin (1861–1949), the founder of *La Revue Wagnérienne* (1885), which was friendly to symbolist writings and *vers libre*.

10 Albert Mockel (1866–1945), a Belgian poet, spread the movement's ideas in his country with the journal *La Wal-*

lonie; his poems were collected in *Chantefable un peu naïve* (1891).

11 Richard Wagner (1813–83) was legendary with the French poets after bringing *Tannhäuser* to Paris in 1861. Mallarmé had written a memoriam in Dujardin's review in 1885, 'Richard Wagner: Rêverie d'un poète français'.

12 *Music and Letters (La Musique et les lettres)*, printed in 1895, was based on a lecture given at Oxford and Cambridge universities in 1894.

W. B. Yeats

William Butler Yeats (1865—1939) was born in Dublin, son of the artist John Butler Yeats. The family circulated impecuniously between London, Dublin and Sligo (the home of his mother's family) 1867—80, then settled in Dublin. In 1885 he began to publish and returned to London in 1887 where he became active in theosophical, mystic and Nationalist circles. In 1889 he met Nationalist crusader Maud Gonne, for him a muse with many faces. In 1891 he helped to found the Rhymers' Club and, in the following year, the Irish Literary Society of Dublin. He spent the summer of 1897 with Lady Gregory, henceforth guide to many things Irish. The first of several American lecture tours took place in 1903. With J. M. Synge and Lady Gregory he directed the Abbey Theatre (1906). He became a member of the Irish Senate (1922) and was awarded the Nobel Prize for Literature (1923). In 1934 he underwent a rejuvenation operation. He died and was buried in France but after the War his body was removed to its final resting place beneath Ben Bulben, Drumcliff, County Sligo.

WRITINGS

Major collections of poetry are: *The Wanderings of Oisin and Other Poems* (1889), *The Wind among the Reeds* (1899), *The Green Helmet and Other Poems* (1910), *The Wild Swans at Coole* (1919), *The Tower* (1928); dramatic works include *At the Hawk's Well* (1916), *The Only Jealousy of Emer* (1918), *Fighting the Waves* (1929), and *Purgatory* (1938); he published a cosmogony, *A Vision* (1925 and 1937).

'The Symbolism of Poetry' was written in 1900 and included in the collection of essays *Ideas of Good and Evil* of 1903.

'A General Introduction for my Work' was written in 1937 for a complete edition which never appeared.

THE SYMBOLISM OF POETRY

I

Symbolism, as seen in the writers of our day, would have no value if it were not seen also, under one 'disguise or another, in every great imaginative writer,' writes Mr Arthur Symons[1] in *The Symbolist Movement in Literature*, a subtle book which I cannot praise as I would, because it has been dedicated to me; and he goes on to show how many profound writers have in the last few years sought for a philosophy of poetry in the doctrine of symbolism, and how even in countries where it is almost scandalous to seek for any philosophy of poetry, new writers are following them in their search. We do not know what the writers of ancient times talked of among themselves, and one bull is all that remains of Shakespeare's talk, who was on the edge of modern times; and the journalist is convinced, it seems, that they talked of wine and women and politics, but never about their art, or never quite seriously about their art. He is certain that no one who had a philosophy of his art, or a theory of how he should write, has ever made a work of art, that people have no imagination who do not write without forethought and afterthought as he writes his own articles. He says this with enthusiasm, because he has heard it at so many comfortable dinner-tables, where someone had mentioned through carelessness, or foolish zeal, a book whose difficulty had offended indolence, or a man who had not forgotten that beauty is an accusation. Those formulas and generalizations, in which a hidden sergeant has drilled the ideas of journalists and through them the ideas of all but all the modern world, have created in their turn a forgetfulness like that of soldiers in battle, so that journalists and their readers have forgotten, among many like events, that Wagner spent seven years arranging and explaining his ideas before he began his most characteristic music; that opera, and with it modern music, arose from certain talks at the house of one Giovanni Bardi[2] of Florence; and that the Pléiade[3] laid the foundations of modern French literature with a pamphlet. Goethe has said, 'a poet needs all philosophy, but he must keep it out of his work', though that is not always necessary; and almost certainly no great art, outside England, where journalists are more powerful and ideas less plentiful than elsewhere, has arisen without a great criticism for its herald or interpreter and protector, and it may be for this reason that great art, now that vulgarity has armed itself and multiplied itself, is perhaps dead in England.

All writers, all artists of any kind, in so far as they have had any philosophical or critical power, perhaps just in so far as they have been deliberate artists at all, have had some philosophy, some criticism of their art; and it has often been this philosophy, or this criticism, that has evoked their most startling inspiration, calling into outer life some portion of the divine life, or of the buried reality, which could alone extinguish in the emotions what their philosophy or their criticism would extinguish in the intellect. They have sought for no new thing, it may be, but only to understand and to copy the pure inspiration of early times, but because the divine life wars upon our outer life, and must needs change its weapons and its movements as we change ours, inspiration has come to them in beautiful startling shapes. The scientific movement brought with it a literature which was always tending to lose itself in externalities of all kinds, in opinion, in declamation, in picturesque writing, in word-painting, or in what Mr Symons has called an attempt 'to build in brick and mortar inside the covers of a book'; and now writers have begun to dwell upon the element of evocation, of suggestion, upon what we call the symbolism in great writers.

II

In 'Symbolism in Painting',[4] I tried to describe the element of
symbolism that is in pictures and sculpture, and described a
little the symbolism in poetry, but did not describe at all the
continuous indefinable symbolism which is the substance of all
style.

There are no lines with more melancholy beauty than these by
Burns:

> The white moon is setting behind the white wave,
> And Time is setting with me, O!

and these lines are perfectly symbolical. Take from them the
whiteness of the moon and of the wave, whose relation to the
setting of Time is too subtle for the intellect, and you take from
them their beauty. But, when all are together, moon and wave
and whiteness and setting Time and the last melancholy cry,
they evoke an emotion which cannot be evoked by any other
arrangement of colours and sounds and forms. We may call this
metaphorical writing, but it is better to call it symbolical writing, because metaphors are not profound enough to be moving,
when they are not symbols, and when they are symbols they are
the most perfect of all, because the most subtle, outside of pure
sound, and through them one can best find out what symbols
are. If one begins the reverie with any beautiful lines that one
can remember, one finds they are like those by Burns. Begin
with this line by Blake:

> The gay fishes on the wave when the moon sucks up the dew;

or these lines by Nash:[5]

> Brightness falls from the air,
> Queens have died young and fair,
> Dust hath closed Helen's eye;

or these lines by Shakespeare:

> Timon hath made his everlasting mansion
> Upon the beached verge of the salt flood;
> Who once a day with his embossed froth
> The turbulent surge shall cover;

or take some line that is quite simple, that gets its beauty from its place in a story, and see how it flickers with the light of the many symbols that have given the story its beauty, as a sword-blade may flicker with the light of burning towers.

All sounds, all colours, all forms, either because of their pre-ordained energies or because of long association, evoke indefinable and yet precise emotions, or, as I prefer to think, call down among us certain disembodied powers, whose footsteps over our hearts we call emotions; and when sound, and colour, and form are in a musical relation, a beautiful relation to one another, they become, as it were, one sound, one colour, one form, and evoke an emotion that is made out of their distinct evocations and yet is one emotion. The same relation exists between all portions of every work of art, whether it be an epic or a song, and the more perfect it is, and the more various and numerous the elements that have flowed into its perfection, the more powerful will be the emotion, the power, the god it calls among us. Because an emotion does not exist, or does not become perceptible and active among us, till it has found its expression, in colour or in sound or in form, or in all of these, and because no two modulations or arrangements of these evoke the same emotion, poets and painters and musicians, and in a less degree because their effects are momentary, day and night and cloud and shadow, are continually making and unmaking mankind. It is indeed only those things which seem useless or very feeble that have any power, and all those things that seem useful or strong, armies, moving wheels, modes of architecture, modes of government, speculations of the reason, would have been a little different if some mind long ago had not given itself to some emotion, as a woman gives herself to her lover, and shaped sounds or colours or forms, or all of these, into a musical relation, that their emotion might live in other minds. A little lyric evokes an emotion, and this emotion gathers others about it and melts into their being in the making of some great epic; and at last, needing an always less delicate body, or symbol, as it grows more powerful, if flows out, with all it has gathered, among the blind instincts of daily life, where it moves a power within powers, as one sees ring within ring in the stem of an old tree. This is maybe what Arthur O'Shaughnessy[6] meant when he made his poets say they had built Nineveh[7] with their sighing; and I am certainly never sure, when I hear of some war, or of some religious excitement, or of some new manufacture, or of anything else that fills the ear of the world, that it has not all happened because of something that a boy piped in Thessaly. I remember once telling a seeress to ask one among the gods who, as she believed, were standing about her in their symbolic bodies, what would come of a charming but seeming trivial labour of a friend, and the form answering, 'the devastation of peoples and the overwhelming of cities.' I doubt indeed if the crude circumstance of the world, which seems to create all our emotions, does more than reflect, as in multiplying mirrors, the emotions that have come to solitary men in moments of poetical contemplation; or that love itself would be more than an animal hunger but for the poet and his shadow the priest, for unless we believe that outer things are the reality, we must believe that the gross is the shadow of the subtle, that things are wise before they become foolish, and secret before they cry out in the marketplace. Solitary men in moments of contemplation receive, as I think, the creative impulse from the lowest of the Nine Hierarchies, and so make and unmake mankind, and even the world itself, for does not 'the eye altering alter all'?

Our towns are copied fragments from our breast;
And all man's Babylons strive but to impart
The grandeurs of his Babylonian heart.

III

The purpose of rhythm, it has always seemed to me, is to prolong the moment of contemplation, the moment when we are both asleep and awake, which is the one moment of creation, by hushing us with an alluring monotony, while it holds us waking by variety, to keep us in that state of perhaps real trance, in which the mind liberated from the pressure of the will is unfolded in symbols. If certain sensitive persons listen persistently to the ticking of a watch, or gaze persistently on the monotonous flashing of a light, they fall into the hypnotic trance; and the rhythm is but the ticking of a watch made softer, that one must needs listen, and various, that one may not be swept beyond memory or grow weary of listening; while the patterns of the artist are but the monotonous flash woven to take the eyes in a subtler enchantment. I have heard in meditation voices that were forgotten the moment they had spoken; and I have been swept, when in more profound meditation, beyond all memory but of those things that come from beyond the threshold of waking life. I was writing once at a very symbolical and abstract poem, when my pen fell on the ground; and as I stooped to pick it up, I remembered some fantastic adventure that yet did not seem fantastic, and then another like adventure, and when I asked myself when these things had happened, I found that I was remembering my dreams for many nights. I tried to remember what I had done the day before, and then what I had done that morning; but all my waking life had perished from me, and it was only after a struggle that I came to remember it again, and as I did so that more powerful and startling life perished in its turn. Had my pen not fallen on the ground and so made me turn from the images that I was weaving into verse, I would never have known that meditation had become trance, for I would have been like one who does not know that he is passing through a wood because his eyes are on the pathway. So I think that in the making and in the understanding of a work of art, and the more easily if it is full of patterns and symbols and music, we are lured to the threshold of sleep, and it may be far beyond it, without knowing that we have ever set our feet upon the steps of horn or of ivory.

IV

Besides emotional symbols, symbols that evoke emotions alone – and in this sense all alluring or hateful things are symbols, although their relations with one another are too subtle to delight us fully, away from rhythm and pattern – there are intellectual symbols, symbols that evoke ideas alone, or ideas mingled with emotions; and outside the very definite traditions of mysticism and the less definite criticism of certain modern poets, these alone are called symbols. Most things belong to one or another kind, according to the way we speak of them and the companions we give them, for symbols, associated with ideas that are more than fragments of the shadows thrown upon the intellect by the emotions they evoke, are the playthings of the allegorist or the pedant, and soon pass away. If I say 'white' or 'purple' in an ordinary line of poetry, they evoke emotions so exclusively that I cannot say why they move me; but if I bring them into the same sentence with such obvious intellectual symbols as a cross or a crown of thorns, I think of purity and sovereignty. Furthermore, innumerable meanings, which are held to 'white' or to 'purple' by bonds of subtle suggestion, and alike in the emotions and in the intellect, move visibly through my mind, and move invisibly beyond the threshold of sleep, casting lights and shadows of an indefinable wisdom on what had seemed before, it may be, but sterility and noisy violence. It is the intellect that decides where the reader shall ponder over the procession of the symbols, and if the symbols are merely emotional, he gazes from amid the accidents and destinies of the world; but if the symbols are intellectual too, he becomes himself a part of pure intellect, and he is himself mingled with the procession. If I watch a rushy pool in the moonlight, my emotion at its beauty is mixed with memories of the man that I have seen ploughing by its margin, or of the lovers I saw there a night ago; but if I look at the moon herself and remember any of her ancient names and meanings, I move among divine people, and things that have shaken off our mortality, the tower of ivory, the queen of waters, the shining stag among enchanted woods, the white hare sitting upon the hilltop, the fool of Faery with his shining cup full of dreams, and it may be 'make a friend of one of these images of wonder', and 'meet the Lord in the air'. So, too, if one is moved by Shakespeare, who is content with emotional symbols that he may come the nearer to our sympathy, one is mixed with the whole spectacle of the world; while if one is moved by Dante, or by the myth of Demeter, one is mixed into the shadow of God or of a goddess. So, too, one is furthest from symbols when one is busy doing this or that, but the soul moves among symbols and unfolds in symbols when trance, or madness, or deep meditation has withdrawn it from every impulse but its own. 'I then saw,' wrote Gérard de Nerval[8] of his madness, 'vaguely drifting into form, plastic images of antiquity, which outlined themselves, became definite, and seemed to represent symbols of which I only seized the idea with difficulty.' In an earlier time he would have been of that multitude whose souls austerity withdrew, even more perfectly than madness could withdraw his soul, from hope and memory, from desire and regret, that they might reveal those processions of symbols that men bow to before altars, and woo with incense and offerings. But being of our time, he has been like Maeterlinck,[9] like Villiers de l'Isle-Adam in *Axël*,[10] like all who are preoccupied with intellectual symbols in our time, a foreshadower of the new sacred book, of which all the arts, as somebody has said, are beginning to dream. How can the arts overcome the slow dying of men's hearts that we call the progress of the world, and lay their hands upon men's heart-strings again, without becoming the garment of religion as in old times?

V

If people were to accept the theory that poetry moves us because of its symbolism, what change should one look for in the manner of our poetry? A return to the way of our fathers, a casting out of descriptions of nature for the sake of nature, of the moral law for the sake of the moral law, a casting out of all anecdotes and of that brooding over scientific opinion that so often extinguished the central flame in Tennyson, and of that vehemence that would make us do or not do certain things; or, in other words, we should come to understand that the beryl stone was enchanted by our fathers that it might unfold the pictures in its heart, and not to mirror our own excited faces, or the boughs waving outside the window. With this change of substance, this return to imagination, this understanding that the laws of art, which are the hidden laws of the world, can alone bind the imagination, would come a change of style, and we would cast out of serious poetry those energetic rhythms, as of a man running, which are the invention of the will with its eyes always on something to be done or undone; and we would seek out those wavering, meditative, organic rhythms, which are the embodiment of the imagination, that neither desires nor hates, because it has done with time, and only wishes to gaze upon some reality, some beauty; nor would it be any longer possible for anybody to deny the importance of form, in all its kinds, for although you can expound an opinion, or describe a thing, when your words are not quite well chosen, you cannot give a body to something that moves beyond the senses, unless your words are as subtle, as complex, as full of mysterious life, as the body of a flower or of a woman. The form of sincere poetry, unlike the form of the 'popular poetry', may indeed be sometimes obscure, or ungrammatical as in some of the best of the *Songs of Innocence and Experience*,[11] but it must have the perfections that escape analysis, the subtleties that have a new meaning every day, and it must have all this whether it be but a little song made out of a moment of dreamy indolence, or some great epic made out of the dreams of one poet and of a hundred generations whose hands were never weary of the sword.

Notes

1 Arthur Symons (1865–1945), poet and critic; his *The Symbolist Movement in Literature* (1899) introduced Yeats to much recent French literature. Yeats had shared quarters in London and travelled to Paris and Ireland with Symons in 1895–6.

2 Giovanni Bardi (1534–1612), Italian musician, writer and scientist. Together with a group known as the Florentine Camerata, he argued against the dominant contrapuntal musical style of the day in favour of the Greek monodic style, preparing the way for the modern opera.

3 The Pléiade was a group of sixteenth-century French writers, among them Joachim Du Bellay and Pierre de Ronsard.

4 'Symbolism in Painting' appeared in 1898.

5 Thomas Nash (or Nashe) (1567–1601), pamphleteer, dramatist, poet and master of 'literary *sansculottisme*' (C. S. Lewis).

6 Arthur O'Shaughnessy (1844–81), poet and playwright, author of *An Epic of Women* (1870), *Lays of France* (1872), *Music and Moonlight* (1874) and *Songs of a Worker* (1881). He worked as a copyist at the British Museum from the age of seventeen.

7 Many fine stone bas-reliefs from Nineveh in Assyria were brought to the British Museum in the 1860s.

8 Gérard de Nerval, pseudonym of Gérard Labrunie (1808–55), French visionary poet and prose writer treated in Symons's *Symbolist Movement*.

9 Maurice Maeterlinck (1862–1949), the Belgian symbolist, was the author of the play *Pelléas et Mélisande* (1892), three

plays for marionnettes (1894) and essays *Le Trésor des humbles* (1896), represented in a chapter 'Maeterlinck as a Mystic' in *The Symbolist Movement in Literature*.

10 Villiers de l'Isle-Adam (1838–89), novelist and playwright. His *Axël* first appeared complete in 1890; for Symons it represented 'a world thought or dreamt in some more fortunate atmosphere than that in which we live'.

11 William Blake's (1757–1827) *The Songs of Innocence* first appeared in 1785, then in 1794 along with *The Songs of Experience*.

A GENERAL INTRODUCTION FOR MY WORK

I *The first principle*

A poet writes always of his personal life, in his finest work out of its tragedy, whatever it be, remorse, lost love, or mere loneliness; he never speaks directly as to someone at the breakfast table, there is always a phantasmagoria. Dante and Milton had mythologies, Shakespeare the characters of English history or of traditional romance; even when the poet seems most himself, when he is Raleigh and gives potentates the lie, or Shelley 'a nerve o'er which do creep the else unfelt oppressions of this earth', or Byron when 'the soul wears out the breast' as 'the sword outwears its sheath', he is never the bundle of accident and incoherence that sits down to breakfast; he has been reborn as an idea, something intended, complete. A novelist might describe his accidence, his incoherence, he must not; he is more type than man, more passion than type. He is Lear, Romeo, Oedipus, Tiresias; he has stepped out of a play, and even the woman he loves is Rosalind, Cleopatra, never The Dark Lady. He is part of his own phantasmagoria and we adore him because nature has grown intelligible, and by so doing a part of our creative power. 'When mind is lost in the light of the Self,' says the Prashna Upanishad, 'it dreams no more; still in the body it is lost in happiness.' 'A wise man seeks in Self', says the Chandogya Upanishad, 'those that are alive and those that are dead and gets what the world cannot give.'[1] The world knows nothing because it has made nothing, we know everything because we have made everything.

II   *Subject-matter*

It was through the old Fenian[2] leader John O'Leary[3] I found my theme. His long imprisonment, his longer banishment, his magnificent head, his scholarship, his pride, his integrity, all that aristocratic dream nourished amid little shops and little farms, had drawn around him a group of young men; I was but eighteen or nineteen and had already, under the influence of *The Faerie Queene* and *The Sad Shepherd*, written a pastoral play, and under that of Shelley's *Prometheus Unbound* two plays, one staged somewhere in the Caucasus, the other in a crater of the moon; and I knew myself to be vague and incoherent. He gave me the poems of Thomas Davis,[4] said they were not good poetry but had changed his life when a young man, spoke of other poets associated with Davis and *The Nation* newspaper, probably lent me their books. I saw even more clearly than O'Leary that they were not good poetry. I read nothing but romantic literature; hated that dry eighteenth-century rhetoric; but they had one quality I admired and admire: they were not separated individual men; they spoke or tried to speak out of a people to a people; behind them stretched the generations. I knew, though but now and then as young men know things, that I must turn from that modern literature Jonathan Swift compared to the web a spider draws out of its bowels; I hated and still hate with an ever growing hatred the literature of the point of view. I wanted, if my ignorance permitted, to get back to Homer, to those that fed at his table. I wanted to cry as all men cried, to laugh as all men laughed, and the Young Ireland poets when not writing mere politics had the same want, but they did not know that the common and its befitting language is the research of a lifetime and when found may lack popular recognition. Then somebody, not O'Leary, told me of Standish O'Grady and his interpretation of Irish legends.[5] O'Leary had sent me to O'Curry,[6] but his unarranged and uninterpreted history defeated my boyish indolence.

A generation before *The Nation* newspaper was founded the Royal Irish Academy had begun the study of ancient Irish literature. That study was as much a gift from the Protestant aristocracy which had created the Parliament as *The Nation* and its school, though Davis and Mitchel[7] were Protestants; was a gift from the Catholic middle classes who were to create the Irish Free State. The Academy persuaded the English Government to finance an ordnance survey on a large scale; scholars, including that great scholar O'Donovan,[8] were sent from village to village recording names and their legends. Perhaps it was the last moment when such work could be well done, the memory of the people was still intact, the collectors themselves had perhaps heard or seen the banshee; the Royal Irish Academy and its public with equal enthusiasm welcomed Pagan and Christian; thought the Round Towers a commemoration of Persian fireworship. There was little orthodoxy to take alarm; the Catholics were crushed and cowed; an honoured great-uncle of mine – his portrait by some forgotten master hangs upon my bedroom wall – a Church of Ireland rector, would upon occasion boast that you could not ask a question he could not answer with a perfectly appropriate blasphemy or indecency. When several counties had been surveyed but nothing published, the Government, afraid of rousing dangerous patriotic emotion, withdrew support; large manuscript volumes remain containing much picturesque correspondence between scholars.

When modern Irish literature began, O'Grady's influence

predominated. He could delight us with an extravagance we were too critical to share; a day will come, he said, when Slieve-na-mon[9] will be more famous than Olympus; yet he was no Nationalist as we understood the word, but in rebellion, as he was fond of explaining, against the House of Commons, not against the King. His cousin, that great scholar Hayes O'Grady,[10] would not join our non-political Irish Literary Society because he considered it a Fenian body, but boasted that although he had lived in England for forty years he had never made an English friend. He worked at the British Museum compiling their Gaelic catalogue and translating our heroic tales in an eighteenth-century frenzy; his heroine 'fractured her heart', his hero 'ascended to the apex of the eminence' and there 'vibrated his javelin', and afterwards took ship upon 'colossal ocean's superficies'. Both O'Gradys considered themselves as representing the old Irish land-owning aristocracy; both probably, Standish O'Grady certainly, thought that England, because decadent and democratic, had betrayed their order. It was another member of that order, Lady Gregory,[11] who was to do for the heroic legends in *Gods and Fighting Men* and in *Cuchulain of Muirthemne* what Lady Charlotte Guest's *Mabinogion*[12] had done with less beauty and style for those of Wales. Standish O'Grady had much modern sentiment, his style, like that of John Mitchel forty years before, shaped by Carlyle; she formed her style upon the Anglo-Irish dialect of her neighbourhood, an old vivid speech with a partly Tudor vocabulary, a syntax partly moulded by men who still thought in Gaelic.

I had heard in Sligo cottages or from pilots at Rosses Point[13] endless stories of apparitions, whether of the recent dead or of the people of history and legend, or that Queen Maeve whose reputed cairn stands on the mountain over the bay. Then at the British Museum I read stories Irish writers of the 'forties and 'fifties had written of such apparitions, but they enraged me more than pleased because they turned the country visions into a joke. But when I went from cottage to cottage with Lady Gregory and watched her hand recording that great collection she has called *Visions and Beliefs* I escaped disfiguring humour.

Behind all Irish history hangs a great tapestry, even Christianity had to accept it and be itself pictured there. Nobody looking at its dim folds can say where Christianity begins and Druidism ends; 'There is one perfect among the birds, one perfect among the fish, and one among men that is perfect.' I can only explain by that suggestion of recent scholars – Professor Burkitt[14] of Cambridge commended it to my attention – that St Patrick came to Ireland not in the fifth century but towards the end of the second. The great controversies had not begun; Easter was still the first full moon after the Equinox. Upon that day the world had been created, the Ark rested upon Ararat, Moses led the Israelites out of Egypt; the umbilical cord which united Christianity to the ancient world had not yet been cut, Christ was still the half-brother of Dionysus. A man just tonsured by the Druids could learn from the nearest Christian neighbour to sign himself with the Cross without sense of incongruity, nor would his children acquire that sense. The organized clans weakened Church organization, they could accept the monk but not the bishop.

A modern man, *The Golden Bough*[15] and *Human Personality*[16] in his head, finds much that is congenial in St Patrick's Creed as recorded in his Confessions, and nothing to reject except the word 'soon' in the statement that Christ will soon judge the quick and the dead. He can repeat it, believe it even, without a thought of the historic Christ, or ancient Judea, or of anything subject to historical conjecture and shifting evidence; I repeat it and think of 'the Self' in the Upanishads. Into this tradition, oral and written, went in later years fragments of Neo-Platonism, cabbalistic words – I have heard the words 'tetragammaton agla'[17] in Doneraile – the floating debris of mediaeval thought, but nothing that did not please the solitary mind. Even the religious equivalent for Baroque and Rococo could not come to us as thought, perhaps because Gaelic is incapable of abstraction. It came as cruelty. That tapestry filled the scene at the birth of modern Irish literature, it is there in the Synge of *The Well of the Saints*,[18] in James Stephens,[19] and in Lady Gregory throughout, in all of George Russell[20] that did not come from the Upanishads, and in all but my later poetry.

Sometimes I am told in commendation, if the newspaper is Irish, in condemnation if English, that my movement perished under the firing squads of 1916; sometimes that those firing squads made our realistic movement possible. If that statement is true, and it is only so in part, for romance was everywhere receding, it is because in the imagination of Pearse[21] and his fellow soldiers the Sacrifice of the Mass had found the Red Branch[22] in the tapestry; they went out to die calling upon Cuchulain:

Fall, Hercules, from Heaven in tempests hurled
To cleanse the beastly stable of this world.

In one sense the poets of 1916 were not of what the newspapers call my school. The Gaelic League, made timid by a modern popularization of Catholicism sprung from the aspidistra and not from the root of Jesse,[23] dreaded intellectual daring and stuck to dictionary and grammar. Pearse and MacDonagh[24] and others among the executed men would have done, or attempted, in Gaelic what we did or attempted in English.

Our mythology, our legends, differ from those of other European countries because down to the end of the seventeenth century they had the attention, perhaps the unquestioned belief, of peasant and noble alike; Homer belongs to sedentary men, even today our ancient queens, our mediaeval soldiers and lovers, can make a pedlar shudder. I can put my own thought, despair perhaps from the study of present circumstance in the light of ancient philosophy, into the mouth of rambling poets of the seventeenth century, or even of some imagined ballad singer of today, and the deeper my thought the more credible, the more peasant-like, are ballad singers and rambling poet. Some modern poets contend that jazz and music-hall songs are the folk art of our time, that we should mould our art upon them; we Irish poets, modern men also, reject every folk art that does not go back to Olympus. Give me time and a little youth and I will prove that even 'Johnny, I hardly knew ye' goes back.

Mr Arnold Toynbee[25] in an annex to the second volume of *The Study of History* describes the birth and decay of what he calls the Far Western Christian culture; it lost at the Synod of Whitby its chance of mastering Europe, suffered final ecclesiastical defeat in the twelfth century with 'the thoroughgoing incorporation of the Irish Christendom into the Roman Church. In the political and literary spheres' it lasted unbroken till the seventeenth century. He then insists that if 'Jewish Zionism and Irish Nationalism succeed in achieving their aims, then Jewry and Irishry will each fit into its own tiny niche . . . among sixty or seventy national communities', find life somewhat easier, but cease to be 'the relic of an independent society . . . the romance of Ancient Ireland has at last come to an end. . . . Modern Ireland has made up her mind, in our generation, to find her level as a willing inmate in our workaday Western world.'

If Irish literature goes on as my generation planned it, it may do something to keep 'Irishry' living, nor will the work of the realists hinder, nor the figures they imagine, nor those described in memoirs of the revolution. These last especially, like certain great political predecessors, Parnell,[26] Swift, Lord Edward,[27] have stepped back into the tapestry. It may be indeed that certain characteristics of the 'Irishry' must grow in importance. When Lady Gregory asked me to annotate her *Visions and Beliefs* I began, that I might understand what she had taken down in Galway, an investigation of contemporary spiritualism. For several years I frequented those mediums who in various poor parts of London instruct artisans or their wives for a few pence upon their relations to their dead, to their employers, and to their children; then I compared what she had heard in Galway, or I in London, with the visions of Swedenborg,[28] and, after my inadequate notes had been published, with Indian belief. If Lady Gregory had not said when we passed an old man in the wood, 'That man may know the secret of the ages', I might never have talked with Shri Purohit Swāmi[29] nor made him translate his Master's travels in Tibet, nor helped him translate the Upanishads. I think I now know why the gamekeeper at Coole heard the footsteps of a deer on the edge of the lake where no deer had passed for a hundred years, and why a certain cracked old priest said that nobody had been to hell or heaven in his time, meaning thereby that the Rath[30] had got them all; that the dead stayed where they had lived, or near it, sought no abstract region of blessing or punishment but re-treated, as it were, into the hidden character of their neighbour-hood. I am convinced that in two or three generations it will become generally known that the mechanical theory has no reality, that the natural and supernatural are knit together, that to escape a dangerous fanaticism we must study a new science; at that moment Europeans may find something attractive in a Christ posed against a background not of Judaism but of Druid-ism, not shut off in dead history, but flowing, concrete, phe-nomenal.

I was born into this faith, have lived in it, and shall die in it; my Christ, a legitimate deduction from the Creed of St Patrick as I think, is that Unity of Being Dante compared to a perfectly proportioned human body, Blake's 'Imagination', what the Upanishads have named 'Self': nor is this unity distant and therefore intellectually understandable, but imminent, differ-ing from man to man and age to age, taking upon itself pain and ugliness, 'eye of newt, and toe of frog'.

Subconscious preoccupation with this theme brought me *A Vision*, its harsh geometry an incomplete interpretation. The 'Irishry' have preserved their ancient 'deposit' through wars which, during the sixteenth and seventeenth centuries, became wars of extermination; no people, Lecky[31] said at the opening of his *Ireland in the Eighteenth Century*, have undergone greater persecution, nor did that persecution altogether cease up to our own day. No people hate as we do in whom that past is always alive, there are moments when hatred poisons my life and I accuse myself of effeminacy because I have not given it adequate expression. It is not enough to have put it into the mouth of a rambling peasant poet. Then I remind myself that though mine is the first English marriage I know of in the direct line, all my family names are English, and that I owe my soul to Shakespeare, to Spenser and to Blake, perhaps to William Morris,[32] and to the English language in which I think, speak, and write, that everything I love has come to me through English; my hatred tortures me with love, my love with hate. I am like the Tibetan monk who dreams at his initiation that he is eaten by a wild beast and learns on waking that he himself is eater and eaten. This is Irish hatred and solitude, the hatred of human life that made Swift write *Gulliver* and the epitaph upon his tomb, that can still make us wag between extremes and doubt our sanity.

Again and again I am asked why I do not write in Gaelic. Some four or five years ago I was invited to dinner by a London society and found myself among London journalists, Indian students, and foreign political refugees. An Indian paper says it was a dinner in my honour; I hope not; I have forgotten, though I have a clear memory of my own angry mind. I should have spoken as men are expected to speak at public dinners; I should have paid and been paid conventional compliments; then they would speak of the refugees; from that on all would be lively and topical, foreign tyranny would be arraigned, England seem even to those confused Indians the protector of liberty; I grew angrier and angrier; Wordsworth, that typical Englishman, had published his famous sonnet to François Dominique Toussaint, a Santo Domingo Negro:[33]

There's not a breathing of the common wind
That will forget thee

in the year when Emmet[34] conspired and died, and he remembered that rebellion as little as the half hanging and the pitch cap that preceded it by half a dozen years. That there might be no topical speeches I denounced the oppression of the people of India; being a man of letters, not a politician, I told how they had been forced to learn everything, even their own Sanskrit, through the vehicle of English till the first discoverer of wisdom had become bywords for vague abstract facility. I begged the Indian writers present to remember that no man can think or write with music and vigour except in his mother tongue. I turned a friendly audience hostile, yet when I think of that scene I am unrepentant and angry.

I could no more have written in Gaelic than can those Indians write in English; Gaelic is my national language, but it is not my mother tongue.

III *Style and attitude*

Style is almost unconscious. I know what I have tried to do, little what I have done. Contemporary lyric poems, even those that moved me – *The Stream's Secret, Dolores*[35] – seemed too long, but an Irish preference for a swift current might be mere indolence, yet Burns may have felt the same when he read Thomson[36] and Cowper.[37] The English mind is meditative, rich, deliberate; it may remember the Thames valley. I planned to write short lyrics or poetic drama where every speech would be short and concentrated, knit by dramatic tension, and I did so with more confidence because young English poets were at that time writing out of emotion at the moment of crisis, though their old slow-moving meditation returned almost at once. Then, and in this English poetry has followed my lead, I tried to make the language of poetry coincide with that of passionate, normal speech. I wanted to write in whatever language comes most naturally when we soliloquize, as I do all day long, upon the events of our own lives or of any life where we can see ourselves for the moment. I sometimes compare myself with the mad old slum women I hear denouncing and remembering; 'How dare you,' I heard one say of some imaginary suitor, 'and you without health or a home!' If I spoke my thoughts aloud they might be as angry and as wild. It was a long time before I had made a language to my liking; I began to make it when I discovered some twenty years ago that I must seek, not as Wordsworth thought, words in common use, but a powerful and passionate syntax, and a complete coincidence between period and stanza. Because I need a passionate syntax for passionate subject-matter I compel myself to accept those traditional metres that have developed with the language. Ezra Pound, Turner,[38] Lawrence wrote admirable free verse, I could not. I would lose myself, become joyless like those mad old women. The translators of the Bible, Sir Thomas Browne,[39] certain translators from the Greek when translators still bothered about rhythm, created a form midway between prose and verse that seems natural to imper- sonal meditation; but all that is personal soon rots; it must be packed in ice or salt. Once when I was in delirium from pneumonia I dictated a letter to George Moore[40] telling him to eat salt because it was a symbol of eternity; the delirium passed, I had no memory of that letter, but I must have meant what I now mean. If I wrote of personal love or sorrow in free verse, or in any rhythm that left it unchanged, amid all its accidence, I would be full of self-contempt because of my egotism and indiscretion, and foresee the boredom of my reader. I must choose a traditional stanza, even what I alter must seem tra- ditional. I commit my emotion to shepherds, herdsmen, camel-drivers, learned men, Milton's or Shelley's Platonist, that tower Palmer drew.[41] Talk to me of originality and I will turn on you with rage. I am a crowd, I am a lonely man, I am nothing. Ancient salt is best packing. The heroes of Shakespeare convey to us through their looks, or through the metaphorical patterns of their speech, the sudden enlargement of their vision, their ecstasy at the approach of death: 'She should have died here-after', 'Of many thousand kisses, the poor last', 'Absent thee from felicity awhile'. They have become God or Mother God-dess, the pelican, 'My baby at my breast', but all must be cold; no actress has ever sobbed when she played Cleopatra, even the shallow brain of a producer has never thought of such a thing. The supernatural is present, cold winds blow across our hands, upon our faces, the thermometer falls, and because of that cold we are hated by journalists and groundlings. There may be in this or that detail painful tragedy, but in the whole work none. I have heard Lady Gregory say, rejecting some play in the modern manner sent to the Abbey Theatre, 'Tragedy must be a joy to the man who dies.' Nor is it any different with lyrics, songs, narra-tive poems; neither scholars nor the populace have sung or read anything generation after generation because of its pain. The maid of honour whose tragedy they sing must be lifted out of history with timeless pattern, she is one of the four Maries, the rhythm is old and familiar, imagination must dance, must be carried beyond feeling into the aboriginal ice. Is ice the correct word? I once boasted, copying the phrase from a letter of my father's, that I would write a poem 'cold and passionate as the dawn'.

When I wrote in blank verse I was dissatisfied; my vaguely mediaeval *Countess Cathleen* fitted the measure, but our Heroic Age went better, or so I fancied, in the ballad metre of *The Green Helmet*. There was something in what I felt about Deirdre, about Cuchulain, that rejected the Renaissance and its charac-teristic metres, and this was a principal reason why I created in dance plays the form that varies blank verse with lyric metres. When I speak blank verse and analyse my feelings, I stand at a moment of history when instinct, its traditional songs and dances, its general agreement, is of the past. I have been cast up out of the whale's belly though I still remember the sound and sway that came from beyond its ribs, and, like the Queen in Paul Fort's ballad,[42] I smell of the fish of the sea. The contrapuntal structure of the verse, to employ a term adopted by Robert Bridges,[43] combines the past and present. If I repeat the first line of *Paradise Lost* so as to emphasize its five feet I am among the folk singers – 'Of mán's first dísobédience ánd the frúit', but speak it as I should cross it with another emphasis, that of passionate prose – 'Of mán's fírst dísobédience and the frúit', or 'Of mán's fírst dísobedience and the frúit'; the folk song is still there, but a ghostly voice, an unvariable possibility, an unconscious norm. What moves me and my hearer is a vivid speech that has no laws except that it must not exorcize the ghostly voice. I am awake and asleep, at my moment of revelation, self-possessed in self-surrender; there is no rhyme, no echo of the beaten drum, the dancing foot, that would overset my balance. When I was a boy I wrote a poem upon dancing that had one good line: 'They snatch with their hands at the sleep of the skies.' If I sat down and thought for a year I would discover that but for certain syllabic limitations, a rejection or acceptance of certain elisions, I must wake or sleep.

The Countess Cathleen could speak a blank verse which I had loosened, almost put out of joint, for her need, because I thought of her as mediaeval and thereby connected her with the general European movement. For Deirdre and Cuchulain and all the other figures of Irish legend are still in the whale's belly.

IV *Whither?*

The young English poets reject dream and personal emotion; they have thought out opinions that join them to this or that political party; they employ an intricate psychology, action in character, not as in the ballads character in action, and all consider that they have a right to the same close attention that men pay to the mathematician and the metaphysician. One of the more distinguished has just explained that man has hitherto slept but must now awake. They are determined to express the factory, the metropolis, that they may be modern. Young men teaching school in some picturesque cathedral town, or settled for life in Capri or in Sicily, defend their type of metaphor by saying that it comes naturally to a man who travels to his work by Tube. I am indebted to a man of this school[44] who went through my work at my request, crossing out all conventional metaphors, but they seem to me to have rejected also those dream associations which were the whole art of Mallarmé. He had topped a previous wave. As they express not what the Upanishads call 'that ancient Self' but individual intellect, they have the right to choose the man in the Tube because of his objective importance. They attempt to kill the whale, push the Renaissance higher yet, out-think Leonardo; their verse kills the folk ghost and yet would remain verse. I am joined to the 'Irishry' and I expect a counter-Renaissance. No doubt it is part of the game to push that Renaissance; I make no complaint; I am accustomed to the geometrical arrangement of history in *A Vision*, but I go deeper than 'custom' for my convictions. When I stand upon O'Connell Bridge in the half-light and notice that discordant architecture, all those electric signs, where modern heterogeneity has taken physical form, a vague hatred comes up out of my own dark and I am certain that wherever in Europe there are minds strong enough to lead others the same vague hatred rises; in four or five or in less generations this hatred will have issued in violence and imposed some kind of rule of kindred. I cannot know the nature of that rule, for its opposite fills the light; all I can do to bring it nearer is to intensify my hatred. I am no Nationalist, except in Ireland for passing reasons; State and Nation are the work of intellect, and when you consider what comes before and after them they are, as Victor Hugo said of something or other, not worth the blade of grass God gives for the nest of the linnet.

Notes

1 The Prashna Upanishad and the Chandogya Upanishad are speculative writings in Sanskrit from after 400 BC, which deal with the nature of the supreme spirit and the means of attaining union with it.

2 The Fenians were a legendary band of Irish warriors led by Finn Mac Cumhaill, raised to defend Ireland against Norse raiders. The nineteenth-century movement, founded in the USA by John O'Mahony, developed in Ireland as the Irish Republican Brotherhood and was aimed at removing English government of the country.

3 John O'Leary (1830–1907), a Fenian leader, author of *Recollections of Fenians and Fenianism* (1896).

4 Thomas Davis (1814–45), Irish politician and poet, and one of the founders of the weekly *The Nation*. His writings formed the gospel of the later Sinn Fein movement.

5 Standish James O'Grady (1846–1928) retold the Irish heroic sagas in *History of Ireland: the Heroic Period* (1878) and *History of Ireland: Cuchulain and His Contemporaries* (1880).

6 Eugene O'Curry (1796–1862), translator of Gaelic manuscripts and author of *On the Manners and Customs of the Ancient Irish* (1873).

7 John Mitchel (1815–75), the Irish nationalist, founded the *United Irishman*.

8 John O'Donovan (1805–61) was a Gaelic scholar.

9 Or Slievenamon, a mountain in Tipperary, legendary site of the Palace of the god Bobd Derg.

10 Standish Hayes O'Grady (1832–1915), an Irish scholar and engineer, compiled Irish manuscripts in the British Museum after living thirty years in California.

11 Lady Isabella Augusta Gregory (1852–1932), an important figure in the Irish literary revival, translated the Irish legends into an Anglo-Irish dialect called 'Kiltartan' in

Cuchulain of Muirthemne (1902) and *Gods and Fighting Men* (1904).

12 Lady Charlotte Guest (1812–95) translated the *Mabinogion* (1838–49).

13 Rosses Point, a district in County Sligo, in western Ireland, where Yeats spent holidays as a child.

14 Francis Crawford Burkitt (1864–1935), English theologian.

15 *The Golden Bough: A Study in Magic and Religion* by Sir James Frazer (1854–1941), published in 12 volumes from 1907–15 and in a one-volume abridged version in 1922.

16 *The Human Personality* (1933) by the English-born American psychiatrist and physician Louis Berg (1901–72).

17 Four consonants in the Hebrew name of God whose utterance was prohibited. In Cabbalistic writings it has a mystical explanation.

18 *The Well of the Saints* (1905) was John Millington Synge's (1871–1909) first play.

19 James Stephens (1882–1950), Irish poet, storyteller and author of *The Crock of Gold* (1912).

20 George Russell (1867–1935) – known as Æ – poet, mystic and founder of *The Irish Statesman* (1923), met Yeats in art school in Dublin.

21 Patrick Henry Pearse (1879–1916), an Irish nationalist who was executed for leading the Easter rising in Dublin in 1916 when he proclaimed the provisional government of the Irish Republic.

22 The Red Branch is a cycle of Gaelic legends, of which the hero is Cuchulain.

23 A tapestry or decoration with a genealogical tree depicting Christ's origin from the 'root of Jesse'.

24 Thomas MacDonagh (1878–1916), an Irish poet and critic shot for his part in the Easter rising of 1916.

25 Arnold Toynbee (1889–1975), the English historian.

26 Charles Stewart Parnell (1846–91), Irish parliamentary

leader. When his relation with Mrs O'Shea became public, he was repudiated by both Gladstone and the Irish party.

27 Lord Edward Fitzgerald (1763–98), Irish military leader. He led an unsuccessful rebellion in which he was wounded and later died.

28 Emanuel Swedenborg (1688–1772), Swedish philosopher, scientist and mystic.

29 Shri Purohit Swāmi was an Indian monk with whom Yeats worked in preparing a translation of the Upanishads in 1935–6.

30 Irish for a hill fort or enclosure, residence of the tribal chief.

31 William Edward Hartpole Lecky (1838–1903), Irish historian and author of *History of Rationalism* and *History of England*.

32 Yeats first met William Morris (1834–96) in 1888.

33 François Dominique Toussaint Louverture (1743–1803) led forces to liberate San Domingo but was captured by the French and died in prison in France.

34 Robert Emmet (1778–1803), Irish revolutionary hero, hanged for his part in the abortive rising against Dublin Castle in 1803. Before reaching the castle, he and his band had murdered the chief justice, Lord Kilwarden.

35 Poems by D. G. Rossetti and A. Swinburne, respectively.

36 James Thomson (1700–48), the Scottish poet and author of *The Seasons*.

37 William Cowper (1731–1800), the English poet and letter-writer.

38 Walter James Redfern Turner (1889–1946), an Australian-born poet, novelist and music critic.

39 Sir Thomas Browne (1605–82), physician and author of *Religio medici* and *Pseudodoxia epidemica*.

40 George Moore (1852–1933), the Irish novelist and playwright.

41 Samuel Palmer (1805–81), the painter and friend of William

Blake. His 'tower' is an illustration in an edition of Milton's *Minor Poems*.

42 Paul Fort (1872–1960), French author of forty volumes of poetry collected as *Ballades françaises*.

43 Robert Seymour Bridges (1844–1930) was poet laureate from 1913 and wrote the critical work *Milton's Prosody* (1921).

44 Ezra Pound (1885–1972). He met Yeats in 1908 and served as his secretary in 1913.

Paul Valéry

Paul Valéry (1871–1945) was born to a family of Corsican and Italian origins in the Mediterranean port of Cette (changed to Sète by the town council in 1927). He studied at Montepellier, from where he made first literary associations around 1890 with Pierre Louÿs, André Gide and Mallarmé. In 1894 he moved to Paris and pursued his interest in scientific and mathematical writings, at the same time working as a correspondent for several literary journals and composing much lyric verse and speculative prose. A taciturn and studious phase from the century's end until 1916 was followed by a period of exuberance which brought forth his best-known works. He inspired much discussion about 'pure poetry' in the 1920s, was elected to the French Academy in 1926 and lectured at the Collège de France in the 1930s and 1940s.

WRITINGS

The most prominent are a study of the mind's workings, *Introduction to the Method of Leonardo da Vinci* (1895); a gnomic prose piece, *An Evening with Monsieur Teste* (1896); a long poem, *la Jeune Parque* (1917); *Album de vers anciens*, collected poems 1890–1900 (1920); further poems, *Charmes* (1922); five volumes of essays, *Variété* (1924–44); and an enormous number of notebooks or *Cahiers* (257 of them) from 1894 until his death ('One need not be Goethe to have an Eckermann,' he wrote of the diary).

'Remarks on Poetry' was given as a lecture in 1927 at the Université des Annales.

REMARKS ON POETRY

Today we have gathered to talk about poetry. The subject is fashionable. It is praiseworthy that, in an age which can be both practical and careless and which, one might feel, is rather distant from all speculative matters, so much interest should be shown not only in poetry itself but also in poetic theory.

Today, therefore, I shall allow myself to be somewhat abstract; in this way, however, I can be brief.

I shall suggest a certain idea of poetry with the firm intention of saying nothing which cannot be confirmed by observation and which everyone could not notice in himself or by himself or at least discover through simple reflection.

I shall begin at the beginning. The beginning of this account of ideas on poetry will have to consider the word itself as it is used in normal discourse. We know that this word has two meanings, that is, two quite different functions. It designates, first of all, a certain kind of emotion, a particular emotive state, which can be aroused by extremely diverse objects or circumstances. We say that a landscape is poetic; we say the same about an event in life or sometimes about a person.

But this term has a second meaning, a much more precise second sense. *Poetry*, in this sense, makes us think of an art, of a strange activity whose aim is to reconstruct the emotion defined by the first meaning of the word.

To reconstitute the poetic emotion at will, outside the natural conditions where it arises spontaneously and by means of the artifices of language – this is the aim of the poet and this is the idea assigned to the second meaning of the word poetry.

The same relations and the same differences exist between these two notions as between the scent of a flower and the work of a chemist who attempts to reconstruct it artificially.

The two ideas are, however, continually confused, with the result that a number of judgements, theories and even works are made ineffectual from the outset by the use of a single word for two quite different things which are, none the less, linked.

Let us speak first about poetic emotion, about the essential emotive state.

You know what most people experience more or less strongly and purely when faced with an imposing natural spectacle. Sunsets, moonlight, forests, the sea, they all move us. Great events, critical moments in the life of the emotions, the trials of love, the evocation of death are so many occasions for, or immediate causes of, inner stirrings of a more or less intense, more or less conscious nature.

This kind of emotion can be distinguished from all other human emotions. But how? For the moment, this is what must be considered. We should contrast as clearly as possible poetic emotion with ordinary emotion. Such a separation is a rather delicate operation since it is never reflected in fact. Tenderness or sadness, wrath or fear or hope are always mingled with essential poetic emotion; and the particular interests and emotions of the individual never fail to combine with that *sense of a universe* which is characteristic of poetry.

I said: *sense of a universe*. I wanted to say that the poetic state or emotion seems to me to consist of a dawning perception, of a tendency to perceive a *world*, or a complete system of relations, in which people, things, events and acts, though they resemble, *each to each*, those which live in and make up the tangible world, the immediate world from which they are taken, stand however in an indefinable though marvellously precise relationship to the modes and laws of our general sensibility. Thus these known objects and people somehow change in value. They communicate with each other and relate quite differently than under ordinary conditions. They become – if you will allow me the expression – *musicalized*, commensurable by virtue of a mutual resonance. Defined in this way, the poetic universe suggests important analogies with the world of dream.

Since this word *dream* has crept into my talk, I should say in passing that in modern times, since Romanticism, an understandable but rather regrettable confusion has arisen between the notion of poetry and that of dream. Neither dream nor reverie is necessarily poetic. They can be poetic; but figures formed *by chance* are harmonious only *by chance*.

None the less, dreaming makes us understand through a common and frequent experience how our consciousness can be invaded, filled, made up by a group of productions which differ remarkably from the mind's ordinary reactions and perceptions. It gives us the familiar example of a *closed world* where all *real* things can be represented, but where everything appears and is modified only by variations in our deep sensibility. The poetic state begins, develops and ends within us in a very similar way. That is, it is thoroughly *irregular, inconstant, involuntary, fragile*, and we lose it as easily as we acquire it – *by accident*. There are times in our life when this emotion and these precious formations do not appear. We do not even think they are possible. Chance gives us them and chance takes them away.

But man is man only through the will and power to preserve or restore what he chooses to remove from the process of natural decay. Thus man has done for this higher emotion what he has done or tried to do for all things which perish and which are regretted. He has sought and found means of fixing and reviving at will his finest or purest states, of reproducing, transmitting and preserving for centuries the formulas of his enthusiasm, his ecstasy, the particular vibrancy of his person; and, as a fortunate and amazing consequence, the invention of these methods of preservation has given him simultaneously the idea and the power to develop and enrich artificially the fragments of poetic life which his nature at times grants him. He has learned to extract from the flux of time, and to detach from circumstances, these marvellous, fortuitous forms and perceptions which would have been lost for ever, had not the ingenious and shrewd being come to the aid of the being of the moment with its inventions for this pure sensing *self*. All arts have been created so as to perpetuate and change, each according to its essence, an ephemeral moment of delight into the certainty of an infinity of delightful moments. *A work is but the instrument of this possible multiplication or reproduction*. Music, painting, architecture are methods whose diversity corresponds to the diversity of the senses. Now, among these means of producing or reproducing a poetic world, of organizing it so that it endures and of amplifying it by conscious work, the most ancient, perhaps the most direct, and certainly the most complex, is language. But by virtue of its abstract nature, its particularly intellectual, that is indirect, effects, and of its practical origins or functions, language sets the artist, concerned with isolating it and ordering it for poetry, a curiously complicated task. There would never have been poets had there been any awareness of the problems to solve. (No one could learn how to walk if, in order to walk, one first had to imagine and grasp as clear ideas all the elements of the smallest step.)

But we are not here to compose verse. On the contrary, we are trying to consider verse as impossible to compose in order to admire with more clarity the efforts of poets, to imagine their temerity and their weariness, their risks and their virtues, and to wonder at their instinct.

Hence I shall attempt to give you in a few words some idea of these difficulties.

I said a moment ago that language is an instrument, a tool, or rather a collection of tools and operations formed by practice and subservient to it. Thus it is a necessarily awkward means which everyone uses, adapts to current needs, alters according to circumstances, adjusts to his physiological make-up and psychological background.

You know what tests we subject it to sometimes. The values and meanings of words, the rules of agreement, pronunciation and spelling are both playthings and instruments of torture. No doubt we pay some attention to the decisions of the Academy;[1] and no doubt teachers, examinations and above all vanity set up certain obstacles to the exercise of individual fancy. In modern

times, moreover, typography acts very powerfully in preserving
these conventions of writing. In this way the effects of private
alterations are delayed somewhat; but the most important qualities of language for the poet, which are obviously, on the one
hand, its musical properties or possibilities and, on the other, its
unlimited signifying values (those which preside over the prop-
agation of ideas derived from one idea), are those least protected
from the caprice, initiative, actions and dispositions of individuals. Each person's pronunciation and individual psychological 'store' introduce into linguistic transmission uncertainty,
the possiblity of misapprehension and an element of surprise –
all of which are quite inevitable. These two points should be
noted: apart from its application to the simplest and commonest
requirements of life, language is quite the opposite of an instrument of precision. And apart from certain very rare coinci-
dences, certain happy combinations of expression and sensible
form, language has no inherent poetic means.

In summary, the poet's bitter and paradoxical destiny obliges
him to make use of a product of everyday, practical language for
exceptional and non-practical ends; he must borrow means of
statistical and anonymous origin in order to accomplish his aim
of exalting and expressing the purest and most individual qualities of his person.

Nothing conveys to us the difficulty of his task better than a
comparison of his initial data with those of the musician. Consider what each has at his disposal when setting to work and
passing from intention to execution.

The fortunate musician! The evolution of his art has provided
him with a privileged position. His means are well defined, the
matter of his composition lies elaborated before him. One can
compare him to a bee when it need only worry about its honey.
The regular combs and wax cells are laid out before it. The bee's
task is clearly measured and confined to the best of itself. And
such is the composer. One can say that music precedes and
awaits him. It has been fully established for a long time!

How was music instituted? In the world of noises we live by the ear. A group of particularly simple noises – that is, easily recognizable by the ear and useful as references – separates itself from the whole: these are the elements whose mutual relations are intuitive; *these exact and remarkable relations are perceived by us as clearly as the elements themselves*. The interval between two notes is as noticeable as a note.

Because of this, these tonal units, these *sounds*, can be put together as successive or simultaneous systems whose structure, sequences, implications, and intersections we perceive and clearly understand. We distinguish clearly between *sound* and *noise*, and we perceive henceforth the contrast of the two. This contrast is an impression of great consequence since it is between the pure and the impure, and points back to that between order and disorder. No doubt it is itself derived from the effects of certain laws of energy. But let us not go so far.

Thus, this analysis of noises, this distinction which made possible the establishment of music as a separate activity and an exploitation of the world of sounds, has been accomplished or at least controlled, unified and codified thanks to the intervention of physical science. Physics itself was discovered at the same time and accepted as a science of measurement. Since antiquity, it has been able to adjust measure to sensation and to obtain the primary result of producing an aural sensation in a constant and identical manner by means of instruments which are, in reality, *measuring instruments*.

The musician thus possesses a perfect group of well-defined means that make sensations correspond exactly with acts; all elements of his activity are available, enumerated and classified for him, and this precise knowledge of his means about which he is instructed and with which he is penetrated and intimately equipped, allows him to foresee and construct without being preoccupied with the subject matter and the general mechanics of his art.

The result is that music possesses a realm absolutely its own.

The world of musical art, a world of sounds, is quite separate from the world of noises. Whereas a noise only evokes some isolated event within us, *a produced sound evokes in itself a whole musical universe*. If in this hall where I am speaking, where you perceive the noise of my voice and of other auditory events, a note were suddenly heard, or if a tuning-fork or a well-tuned instrument began to vibrate, then, only just affected by this exceptional noise, *which cannot be confused with the others*, you would immediately have the sensation of a *beginning*. A completely different atmosphere would be created instantaneously, a special state of anticipation would be felt, a new order, a *world*, would be announced and your attention would be fixed upon receiving it. Moreover, your attention would somehow tend by itself to develop these premises and to anticipate further sensations of the same kind and of the *same purity* as the first.

And the counter-proof exists.

If, in a concert hall, while the symphony reverberates and dominates, a chair should fall, a person should cough or a door be slammed, we immediately sense some sort of rupture. Something indefinable like a charm or a crystal has been broken or cracked.

Now, this atmosphere, this powerful and fragile charm, this universe of sounds, is available to every composer by the nature of his art and the assets that go with the art.

The poet's equipment is quite different and infinitely less fortunate. Pursuing a goal which is not excessively different from the musician's, he is deprived of the immense advantages I have just noted. He must create or re-create at every moment what the other finds ready made and ready to use.

In what an unfavourable, disordered state the poet finds things! Before him is this everyday language, this assembly of means so coarse that all knowledge which aims at precision rejects them so as to create its own instruments of thought; he must borrow this collection of terms and traditional, irrational rules, modified by everyone, introduced, interpreted and codified with little logic. There is nothing less in keeping with the goals of the artist than this essential disorder from which he must continually extract the elements of the order he wishes to produce. For the poet, there has been no physicist to determine the constant properties of these elements of his art, their relations and the conditions of their identical emission. No tuning-forks, metronomes, no inventors of scales, and no theoreticians of harmony. No certainty unless it be that of the semantic and phonetic fluctuations of the language. And in no way does this language act, like sound, upon a single sense, the sense of hearing, which is, more than any other, the sense of anticipation and attention. On the contrary, it forms a mixture of perfectly incoherent sensory and mental stimuli. Each word is an instantaneous collection of unrelated effects. Each word couples a sound and a meaning. I'm mistaken: there are at once many sounds and many meanings. *Many sounds*, as many as there are provinces in France and, almost, as there are people in each province. This is a very serious circumstance for the poets whose intended musical effects are confused or distorted by the action of their readers. *Many meanings*, since the images each word suggests to us are generally rather different and their secondary images infinitely different.

Language is a complex thing, a combination of properties at once effectively bound and independent by nature and function. A discourse may be logical and full of meaning, though without rhythm and measure; it may be agreeable to the ear and perfectly absurd or meaningless; it may be clear and empty, vague and delightful. . . . But in order to be aware of its strange multiplicity, it suffices to enumerate all the sciences created to cater for this diversity, each for exploiting one of its elements. One may study a text in many independent ways, for it is of equal interest to phonetics, semantics, syntax, logic, rhetoric, as well as metrics and etymology.

This, then, is the poet at grips with this all-too-impure, inconstant material, bound to speculate on the sound and sense in turn, to meet the demands not only of harmony, of the musical phrase, but also of various intellectual conditions such as logic, grammar, the poem's subject, all kinds of figures and ornaments, not to mention conventional rules. See what an effort is implied by attempting to bring a discourse to a satisfactory conclusion, for which so many requirements must be miraculously met at the same time.

The uncertain and minute workings of literary art begin here. But this art has two aspects, two fundamental modes which are opposed in their radical state, but which, nevertheless, meet and are linked by a host of intermediate degrees. There is *prose* and there is *verse*. Between them are all the mixtures of the two; but today I shall consider them in their radical states. One might illustrate this opposition of the extremes by exaggerating it somewhat: one might say that the limits of language are *music*, on one hand, and *algebra*, on the other.

I shall make use of a comparison I have used before in order to clarify my thoughts on this subject. One day when I was speaking on the same topic in a foreign city and had just used this comparison, one of my listeners gave me a remarkable quotation, which made me realize that the idea was not new, though it was at least to me.

Here is the quotation. It is an excerpt from a letter from Racan[2] to Chapelain,[3] in which Racan tells us that Malherbe[4] likened prose to walking and poetry to dancing, as I shall do in a moment:

Give whatever name you please to my prose – galant, naïve or playful. I am resolved to observe the precepts of my first master Malherbe, and never to look for number or cadence in my periods, nor for any other ornament than the clarity which can express my thoughts. This good man (Malherbe) compared prose to ordinary walking and poetry to dancing, and he used to say that in the things we are obliged to do we must tolerate some negligence, but in the things we do out of vanity it is ridiculous to be no more than mediocre. The lame and the gouty cannot avoid walking, but nothing obliges them to dance the waltz or the cinquepace.

The comparison which Racan attributes to Malherbe, and which I, for my part, had easily perceived, is direct. I want to show that it is fruitful. It develops at length with a curious precision. Perhaps it is something more than an apparent like-ness.

Walking, like prose, always has a precise object. It is an act directed *toward* some object which we aim to reach. The actual circumstances, the nature of the object, the need I have of it, the impulse of my desire, the state of my body and that of the ground, determine the nature of walking, prescribe its direc-tion, speed and ending. All the properties of walking derive from these instantaneous conditions which combine on each occasion in a *new way*, so that no two strides are exactly alike, and each time there is a special creation, which is each time abolished as though absorbed in the completed act.

Dancing is something quite different. It is without doubt a system of acts which are, at the same time, ends in themselves. Dancing goes nowhere. If it pursues something, it is only an ideal object, a state, a pleasure, the ghost of a flower or some self-centred ecstasy, an extremity of life, a summit, a supreme point of being. . . . As different as dance is from utilitarian movement, this essential though infinitely simple observation should be noted: *that it uses the same limbs, the same organs, bones, muscles and nerves as walking itself.*

Exactly the same is true of poetry which uses the same words, forms and tones as prose.

Thus prose and poetry are distinguished by the difference of certain laws or momentary conventions of movement and func-tion, applied to identical elements and mechanisms. That is why one must avoid thinking of poetry as one does of prose. What is true of one has no meaning in many cases when one seeks it in the other. And this is why (to give an example) it is easy to justify the use of inversions; for these alterations of the customary and, in some ways, elementary order of words in French have been criticized in various periods, very superficially to my mind, for reasons which can be summed up by this unacceptable formula: poetry is prose.

Let us continue a bit with the comparison which can bear further scrutiny. A man is walking. He moves from one place to another along a path which is always the path of least action. Here we note that poetry would be impossible if it were subjected to the rule of the straight line. One is taught: 'Say it is raining if you mean it is raining!' But the object of the poet is not and can never be to let us know that it is raining. There is no need for a poet to tell us to take our umbrella. Look what would happen to Ronsard and Hugo, to the rhythm, images and consonances of the finest verses in the world if poetry were subjected to the 'Say it is raining' system! It is only by a clumsy confusion of genres and circumstance that one can reprove a poet for his indirect expressions and complex forms. One overlooks the fact that poetry implies a decision to change the function of language.

I return to the man walking. When this man has completed his movement, when he has reached the spot, the book, the fruit, the object he desired, this possession immediately cancels his whole act, the effort consumes the cause, the end absorbs the means, and, whatever the ways and means of his act and his step, only the result remains. Once the lame or the gouty, whom Malherbe mentioned, have painfully reached the armchair which was their goal, they are no less seated than the alertest of men who might reach the chair in one sprightly step. The same is true of the use of prose. Once the language I have been using – which has expressed my aim, my desire, my command, my opinion, my request or my answer – fulfils its task, it vanishes almost as soon as it arrives. I sent it off to perish, to be transformed irrevocably in you, and I shall know that I was *understood* by the remarkable fact that my discourse no longer exists. It is entirely and definitively replaced by its *meaning* or at least by a certain meaning, that is, by the images, impulses, reactions or acts of the person to whom one speaks; in short, by an inner modification or reorganization of the person. But one who has not understood preserves and *repeats the words*. The experience is simple. . . .

Thus you see that the perfection of that discourse, whose sole destination is comprehension, consists evidently in the facility with which it is transmuted into a quite different thing, into non-language. If you have understood my words, my words themselves are no longer of any importance to you; they have disappeared from your minds while you possess, none the less, their counterpart, you possess in the form of ideas and relationships the means for restoring the meaning of these remarks, *in a form which may be quite different*.

In other words, in practical or abstract uses of language which is specifically *prose*, the form is not preserved, does not survive understanding, but dissolves in clarity, for it has acted, has made itself understood, has lived.

But the poem, on the contrary, does not die for having been of use; it is expressly made to be reborn from its ashes, perpetually to be again what it has been.

Poetry may be recognized by this remarkable effect which could well serve as a definition: that it tends to reproduce itself in its form and that it asks to be reconstructed just as it was. If I were thinking in terms of industrial technology, I would say that poetic form is recuperated automatically.

This is an admirable and singularly characteristic property. I should like to give you a simple illustration of this. Imagine a pendulum which swings between two symmetrical points. Associate with one of these points the idea of rhythmic force, syllabic sonority, the physical act of speaking and the fundamental psychological surprises caused by unusual word combinations. And with the other point, the conjugate point, associate the intellectual effect, the visions and feelings which for you make up the 'content' and the 'meaning' of the given poem, and then observe that the movement of your mind or of your attention, once it is given over to poetry, is obedient and submissive to the successive impulses of the language of the gods, moves from the *sound* to the *sense*, from the container to the contained, everything taking place at first as in ordinary speech; but then, at each line, the living pendulum is brought back to its verbal and musical point of departure. The sense that is suggested finds its only expression, its only form, in the very form from which it emerged. Thus, between the form and the content, the sound and the sense, the poem and the state of poetry, an oscillation is described, a symmetry, an *equality of value* and of power.

This harmonious exchange between the impression and the expression is, to my mind, the essential principle of poetic mechanics, that is, of the production of the poetic state through speech. The poet's profession is to find fortuitously and to seek industriously those singular forms of language whose action I have tried to analyse for you.

Understood thus, poetry differs radically from all prose: in particular, it is clearly opposed to description and narration of events, which tend to give the illusion of reality, that is, to the novel and the story, when their aim is to impart the power of truth to narratives, portraits, scenes and other representations of real life. This difference even has physical signs which are easily observed. Compare the attitude of the novel reader with that of the poetry reader. They might be the same person but the former differs entirely when he reads one or the other work. Look at the novel reader when he plunges into the imaginary life the book brings him. His body no longer exists. He holds his head in his hands. He is, he moves, he acts and he suffers only in the mind. He is absorbed by what he is devouring; he cannot restrain himself, for some sort of demon urges him on. He wants the continuation and the end, he is prey to a kind of alienation:

he participates, triumphs, grows sad, he is no longer himself, he is only a brain separated from its outer forces, that is, given over to its images, passing through a sort of *crisis of credulity*.

The poetry reader is quite different.

If poetry truly acts on someone, it is surely not by dividing him in his nature, by communicating him illusions of a fictitious and purely mental life. Poetry imposes upon him no false reality which requires the submission of the mind and thus the abstention of the body. Poetry must extend over the whole being; it excites the muscular organization with rhythms, delivers or unleashes the verbal faculties and exalts all this activity; poetry orders the depths of our being, for it aims to provoke or reproduce the unity and harmony of the living person, an extraordinary unity which manifests itself when a man is possessed by an intense feeling which leaves none of his powers unaffected.

All things considered, the difference between the action of the poem and that of an ordinary narrative is physiological in nature. The poem unfolds in a richer region of our functions of movement, it requires our participation in a form that is nearer to complete action, whereas the story or the novel transforms us more into slaves of dream and of our faculty of being hallucinated.

But I repeat that innumerable degrees and transitional forms lie between these extreme limits of literary expression.

Having tried to define the realm of poetry, I ought now to try to consider the poet's actual work, the problems of composition and production. But this would take us down a prickly path. Innumerable torments wait here, disputes which cannot be resolved, trials, enigmas, cares and even despairs, which make the poet's occupation one of the most uncertain and most exhausting that exist. The same Malherbe I have already quoted said that after completing a good sonnet the author had the right to ten years of rest. By this he implied even more, that the words, a *completed sonnet*, meant something. . . . For my part, I hardly understand them. . . . I translate them as an *abandoned sonnet*.

However, let us touch on this difficult question: the making of verse. . . . But you all know that there is a very simple way of making verse.

It suffices to be *inspired*, and things take care of themselves. Indeed I wish it were like this. Life would be bearable. Let us accept, though, this naïve belief and consider its consequences.

Whoever is satisfied with it must agree either that poetic production is a result of pure chance or that it proceeds from some sort of supernatural communication; both hypotheses reduce the poet to a miserably passive role. Both make him either a sort of *urn* in which millions of marbles are shaken, or a *talking table* animated by a spirit. Table or vase, in fact, but no god – the opposite of a god, the opposite of a Self.

And the unfortunate author who is thus no longer an author but a signatory, responsible in the same way as a newspaper editor, is bound to say to himself: 'In your works, dear poet, what is good is obviously not yours, and what is bad could only be yours.'

It is odd that more than one poet has been satisfied – unless he had not grown proud – to be no more than an instrument, a temporary *medium*.

Now, both experience and reflection show us, on the contrary, that those poems whose complex perfection and successful development most forcefully give their amazed readers the notion of a miracle, a stroke of luck, a superhuman accomplishment (owing to an extraordinary collection of virtues that one may wish but not hope to find brought together in a work), are also masterpieces of labour, are, as well, monuments of intelligence and sustained work, products of will and analysis, demanding qualities too multifarious to be reduced to those of a machine for recording enthusiasms or ecstasies. Faced with a beautiful poem of some length, one feels that the chances are infinitesimal that a man might improvise the lot, with no other effort than that of writing or dictating what comes to his mind: a singularly self-assured discourse, furnished with continuous resources, constant harmony and an uninterrupted flow of felicitous ideas, a discourse which never fails to charm, in which there are no accidents, no signs of weakness or failing powers, none of those vexing incidents which destroy the spell and ruin the poetic universe of which I was just speaking.

It is not that something more is not needed to be a poet, some *virtue* which is irreducible, which cannot be analysed as definable actions and hours of work. *Pegasus-power* and *Pegasus-hours* are not yet legal units of poetic force.

There is a special quality, a sort of individual *energy* proper to the poet. It appears to him and reveals him to himself in certain infinitely precious moments.

But these are only moments and this superior energy (in so far, that is, as all other human energies cannot make up or replace it) *can exist and act only in brief and fortuitous manifestations*.

One must add – and this is rather important – that the treasures that this energy illuminates in our mind's eye, the ideas or the forms it produces within us, are far from having the same value in the eyes of others.

These infinitely precious moments, these moments which lend a kind of universal dignity to the relations and intuitions they provoke, are no less productive of illusory or incommunicable values. *What is valuable to us alone is worth nothing*. This is the law of Literature. These sublime states are in truth *absences* in which natural wonders, which are found only there, converge; but these wonders are always impure, I mean mixed with base or barren things, insignificant or incapable of withstanding outer light, or impossible to retain or preserve. In the glare of exaltation, all that shines is not gold.

In summary, certain moments betray to us depths where the best of ourselves reside – though only as particles active within formless matter, as fragments of a peculiar or coarse shape. Thus one must separate these elements of noble metal from the mass and make sure they are fused together and used for fashioning an ornament.

If one were to develop rigorously the doctrine of pure inspiration, one would arrive at quite strange conclusions. One would necessarily find, for example, that a poet who limits himself to transmitting what he receives, and to passing on to unknown readers what he gathers from the unknown, has no need to understand what he writes under mysterious dictation.

He does not act upon this poem of which he is not the source. He can be quite extraneous to what flows through him. This inevitable consequence makes me think of what once was generally believed about demonic possession. One reads in old documents which tell of inquests into witchcraft that people were often proved to be possessed by the devil and, though ignorant and uncultured, were condemned for having dicussed, argued and blasphemed during their attacks before their terrified interrogators in Greek, Latin and even Hebrew. (I doubt this Latin was learned the easy way!)

Is this what is required of the poet? Certainly, an emotion characterized by the powerful, spontaneous expression which it unleashes is the essence of poetry. But the poet's task cannot consist merely in being content to undergo it. These expressions, springing from emotion, are only *pure* by accident, they bring with themselves many things of an inferior quality, they contain many faults whose effect is to frustrate poetic development and interrupt the prolonged resonance that is to be produced in another's soul. For the poet's desire, if he aims at the highest of his art, can only be to introduce some other soul into the divine duration of his harmonious life, in which all forms are composed and measured, and *responses* are exchanged between all his sensory and rhythmic powers.

Inspiration, however, belongs to and is destined for the reader, just as the poet's task is to make one think about it and believe in it, to do what is necessary so that one attributes only to the gods a work that is too perfect or too moving to be the product of a man's uncertain hands. The object itself of art and the principle of its artifice is precisely to communicate the impression of an ideal state in which the man who should possess it will be able to produce spontaneously, effortlessly and indefatigably a magnificent and marvellously ordered expression of his nature and of our destinies.

Notes

1 From 1634 the function of the French Academy has been to oversee the French language by publishing grammars and a dictionary (eight editions between 1694 and 1932).

2 Honorat de Bueil, Seigneur de Racan (1589–1670). From 1605 a friend and pupil of Malherbe, and an early member of the French Academy.

3 Jean Chapelain (1595–1674), a founding member of the French Academy, an unsuccessful poet but an influential man of letters.

4 François de Malherbe (1555–1628) turned against the poetic practices of the Pléiade group, stressing purity of language and adherence to prosodic rules.

Hugo von Hofmannsthal

Hugo von Hofmannsthal (1874–1929) was born into a wealthy Viennese family. Under the pen-name 'Loris', he wrote exquisite verse while still at school. He studied Romance philology at Vienna University where he wrote but did not submit a thesis on Victor Hugo (1901), deciding against an academic career. After his marriage in 1902 he settled in Rodaun, on the outskirts of Vienna, and in 1906 he began his long association as a librettist with Richard Strauss. With Max Reinhard and others, he launched the Salzburg Festival after the War.

WRITINGS

These include poems and lyrical dramas from 1891, *Gestern* (*Yesterday*, 1891), *Der Tor und der Tod* (*The Fool and Death*, 1893), *Das Bergwerk zu Falun* (*The Mine at Falun*, 1899); *Selected Poems* (1903); the libretto of *Der Rosenkavalier* (1911); *Jedermann* (*Everyman*, adapted from the English morality play, 1911); a social comedy, *Der Schwierige* (*The Difficult Man*, 1921); a tragedy, *Der Turm* (*The Tower*, after Calderón's *Life Is a Dream*, 1923; a second version in 1927); a fragmentary novel, *Andreas* (published posthumously); and shorter prose fiction.

'Poetry and Life' was part of a lecture and first appeared in the Viennese newspaper *Die Zeit* in 1896, signed 'Loris'.

'Three Short Reflections' was printed in 1921 in the *Neue Freie Presse*, Vienna.

POETRY AND LIFE

You have invited me here to tell you something about a poet of this age or about several poets or about poetry in general. You listen willingly, I assume, to what I enjoy speaking about; we are all young and so it would seem that there is nothing more fitting nor more harmless. I suppose it would not be very difficult for me to assemble several hundred adjectives and verbs which might divert you for a quarter-hour; I believe this to be true principally because we are all young and I can imagine more or less the tune you like to dance to. It is rather easy to ingratiate oneself with one's own generation. 'We' is a nice word, the lands of our contemporaries curl up like an enormous background right to the sea, indeed to the stars, and a variety of pasts lie underfoot, deposited in transparent chasms like captives. There are many agreeable and spurious ways to discourse on contemporary poetry. And you especially are accustomed to hearing about the arts. Your memory stores an incredible number of slogans and proper names, and they all mean something for you. You have come along so far that nothing at all displeases you any more. I should conceal from you, of course, that most names mean nothing, absolutely nothing, for me; that I am not in the least satisfied with what these names imply. I should conceal from you that I have come seriously to appreciate that one should hardly ever speak of art in general, that one can hardly speak of art, that only the unessential and worthless aspects of art, because of their explicitness, lend themselves to discussion; and, because of this, one says less and less the deeper one has penetrated the interior recesses of the arts. Thus I should mislead you in regard to the great difference in our ways of thinking. But the spring outside and the city in which we live with the many churches and gardens and the great variety of people, and the singular, deceptive, affirmative element of life would come to my aid with so many colourful veils that you would believe that I have been sacrificing with you when I have been sacrificing against you and you would praise me.

On the other hand I feel I could easily feign to share – as an unexpected, somewhat entertaining antithesis – your tastes and aesthetic habits. But whether you smile at my attempt to discuss some such topic with knowing smiles, with the smiles of experienced readers of literary supplements, or whether you listen to me with suppressed aversion, I would under no circumstance flatter myself that I might be understood by you – under no circumstance would I assume that you might take any notice of my opinions except for the sake of form and appearance. I would be assailed with arguments which have nothing to do with me and defended with arguments which are not to the point. I would appear helpless like an inexperienced child at times and then at other times like an old man beyond understanding: all of this in the area of my own expertise, in the only subject I can possibly know anything about. Then of course good manners would inhibit you from shifting the argument to another subject quite beyond my grasp, like history or social history or sociology. But in my own little field I would oblige you to fight with heavy weapons against what I know to be scarecrows and to struggle across streams which I reckon to be eternal limits, as deep as the Abyss, as mighty as death. I would be filled with the greatest distrust, however, if by chance you were to agree with me; then I would be doubly convinced that you had taken figuratively everything I meant literally or that some misunderstanding had occurred.

All praise I can bestow upon the poet will appear wanting to you: across a wide gulf of silence it will sound sparse and insubstantial. Your reviewers and critics will fill their mouths full, like water-spewing tritons, when they praise: but their praise is directed at parts and fragments, mine at the whole, their amazement at the relative, mine at the absolute.

I believe that the concept of the whole in art has been lost generally. Nature and imitation have been thrown together to yield a hybrid thing, like a panorama or a shelf of wax statues.

The concept of poetry has been degraded to that of an embellished confession. Certain words of Goethe of too subtle a figurativeness to be understood by biographers and glossarists have brought about a terrible confusion. One recalls the dangerous similarities between the occasional poem and the poem 'written straight from the soul'. I know nothing more like a panorama than the way in which *Werther* is portrayed in the biographies of Goethe,[1] with those impudent declarations of how far experience goes and where imagination takes over. In this way a new sense-organ has been created with which to savour formlessness. The decay of the spiritual in art has been brought on jointly by philologists, journalists and poetasters. That today we understand one another so little that I am able to speak to you less easily about a poet in your times and of your language than an English traveller could about the customs and opinions of an Asiatic civilization – this fact arises out of a great heaviness and ugliness introduced into our culture by a number of dust-feeding intellectuals.

Subjected to all the tiresome chatter about individuality, style, sentiment, mood, and so on, you have perhaps forgotten that the material of poetry is words, that a poem is a weightless weaving of words which through their ordering, their sound and their content call forth a precisely transcribed, illusively distinct, fleeting soul state which we call mood, in that they join the memory of the visible and the memory of the audible with the principle of movement. If you can discover for yourself this definition of the least perceptible of arts, you will feel as though you have cast aside a bewildering burden on the conscience. Words are everything, those words with which things seen and heard can be called up to a new existence, those which, following inspired laws, can animate this existence. There is no path that leads directly from poetry to life; from life, none that leads directly to poetry. The word which carries life's substance and its dream-like brother-word, which can stand in a poem, strive separately and float unknowingly by one another like the two pails of a well. No external law forbids casuistry in art, forbids any sort of squabbling with life, any immediate reference to life or any direct imitation of life; the only thing it forbids is simple impossibility: those heavy things which are as unlikely here as cows are in the tops of trees.

'Meaning does not decide' – I am using the words of an author I don't know but whom I respect – 'meaning does not decide the value of poetry (otherwise it would be a sort of wisdom or erudition); rather the form (i.e. something which is in no way external), that profoundly stirring quality of metre and sound, decides its value; and it is this value which in every age has distinguished the original artists, the masters, from the derivative artists, those of a second order. Nor is the value of poetry determined by the single, if felicitous, discovery of a line, a stanza or a larger unit. The combination, the relation of the separate parts to one another, the necessary sequence of things, all this characterizes lofty poetry.'

I will add two observations which are virtually self-evident.

Both rhetoric, which views life as raw material, and meditations in solemn speech have no right to the name of poetry.

The success of the only determining factor, the choice of words and their necessary arrangement (rhythm), will be judged by the artist's ability with metre and a reader's receptiveness to it.

This, which alone forms the essence of poetry, is what is most ignored. There is no element in any art style I know of which is more outrageously neglected than the adjective in the recent so-called poetry by German writers. It is either used thoughtlessly or with an intentional garishness which undermines everything else. However, the deficiency of rhythmic feeling is even more annoying. Apparently everyone has forgotten that this is the lever of all activity. One poet would be elevated above all other German writers of the last decades if it could be said that his adjectives are not still-born and his rhythms nowhere belie his intentions.

Every rhythm carries in itself the invisible line of that movement which it can evoke; if the rhythms grow torpid, the
concealed gesture of passion in them is being submitted to
tradition; the rhythms which make up typical, insignificant
ballets are like this.

I find it difficult to conceive of 'personalities' who have no
individual sound, whose inner movements make do with casual
rhythm. I can no longer listen to their Uhland,[2] their Eichendorff[3] metres, and envy no one whose uncouth ears still can.

The individual sound is everything; whoever fails to maintain
it forgoes the inner freedom which can first make the work
possible. The most valiant and powerful poet is he who can
arrange his words most freely, for there is nothing so difficult as
tearing them away from their fixed, false combinations. A new
and bold combination of words is the most wonderful gift to the
soul, nothing less than a sculpture of the youth Antinoüs[4] or a
huge arched gate.

We should be allowed to be artists in words as others are in
white and coloured stone, in metals, in purified sounds or in
dance. We should be valued for our art, the rhetoricians for their
conviction and force, the teachers of wisdom for their wisdom,
the mystics for their illumination. If, on the other hand, one
wants confessions, these can be found in the memoirs of states-
men and littérateurs, in the autobiographies of physicians,
dancers, opium-eaters: for people who do not know how to
differentiate the material from the art, art is simply not available; but of course enough has been written for their needs.

I surprise you. You are deceived and think I am driving the
life out of poetry for you.

You are surprised that a poet praises the rules to you and sees
the whole of poetry in word sequence and metre. But there are
more than enough dilettantes to praise intentions and enough
servants with lugubrious minds to attend to what is quite worthless. Don't be anxious: I will give life back to you. I know what
life should make of art. I love life; even more – I love nothing but

life. But I do not love people who wish to put ivory teeth into painted men and who place marble statues on the stone benches of a garden as if they were people out for a walk. You must give up the habit of asking writers to write with red ink so as to make believe they write with blood.

I have spoken to you too much about function and too little about soul. Indeed, I hold function to be the soul of art, its soul and body, its seed and shell, its whole, entire being. If it were not functional, its purpose would be obscure. But if its function were determined by life, by its own material content, its purpose would be equally obscure. It has been said that a reciprocal tendency can be seen in the arts, a tendency of one art to abandon its own sphere of activity and yield to the activity of a related art: music clearly distinguishes itself as the common goal of all such striving for something else, since it is the art in which content is virtually eliminated.

Poetry's principle is a spiritual one – that of floating, endlessly equivocal words, suspended between God and creature. An aesthetically minded school of poetry of a half-vanished age was guilty of a good deal of stiffness and narrow-mindedness in labouring the comparison of poems to hewn stone, busts, jewels and buildings.[5]

But this shows why poems are like plain but enchanted beakers, in which each of us sees the wealth of his soul – in which, however, impoverished souls see almost nothing.

Beginning with the Vedas and the Bible, all poems can be apprehended only by people who are alive. A cut stone, a beautiful fabric, will always be available, but a poem, perhaps once in a lifetime. A great sophist has accused all the poets of this age with not knowing enough about the fervour of words. But what do people of this age know about the fervour of life! Those who do not know about loneliness, society, pride, humility, weakness and strength – how could they perceive the tokens of loneliness and humility and strength in poetry? The more eloquently one can speak and the more one is overcome by the illusion of thought, the greater the distance from the beginnings of the paths to life. And only by walking these paths, by experiencing the weariness of their chasms and the weariness of their peaks, does one gain an understanding of spiritual art. But the paths are so long and the unending experiences along them consume one another so inexorably that the meaninglessness of any explanation or any persuasion weighs upon the heart like a fatal and yet god-like paralysis; and those who truly understand fall silent again like those who truly create.

You have invited me to talk to you about a poet. But I can tell you nothing his poems could not tell you about himself, about other poets, or about poetry in general. To know what the sea is one must at least venture to ask the fish. At the very most, one learns from them that it is not made of wood.

Notes

1 Johann Wolfgang von Goethe (1749–1832) published *Die Leiden des jungen Werthers* (*The Sorrows of Young Werther*) in 1774. Since it concerns a young man's unrequited love for a married woman and consequent suicide, the parallels with Goethe's own relation to a married woman Charlotte Buff at the time (along with other parallels between novel and life) are frequently recorded by the biographers and literary historians.

2 Ludwig Uhland (1787–1862), German poet, and author of epics, historical ballads and romances.

3 Joseph von Eichendorff (1788–1857) wrote Romantic lyric poetry, much in the popular rhythms of folksong.

4 A beautiful youth, the favourite of the emperor Hadrian in the second century AD, and widely represented on coins and in statues as ideal youthful beauty.

5 This refers to the French Parnassian school grouped around Théophile Gautier (1811–72), Leconte de Lisle (1818–94)

and Théodore de Banville (1823–91), whose poetry stressed precision in description and drew somewhat on the positivist sciences of the day.

THREE SHORT REFLECTIONS

The irony of things

Long before the war I came across this observation in Novalis's *Fragments*:[1] 'After an unhappy war comedies must be written.' This note, in its peculiarly laconic form, was rather puzzling to me. Today I understand it better. The principle of comedy is irony, and in fact nothing is better able than an unhappily concluded war to make the irony that rules all things on earth evident to us. Tragedy lends its hero, the individual, artificial value: it makes him a demigod and elevates him above domestic circumstance. If it wanders only a half-step from this unconscious but necessary tradition, it passes into the sphere of comedy: a play such as *Hamlet* almost goes this far – but Hamlet himself is still a king and a hero, though one whose substance is consumed by self-irony and the irony of circumstances, like a snowman exposed to the sun; and domestic tragedy is quite nonsensical in that the world it would portray is one of social determinants; tragedy, by contrast, grows out of what is socially undetermined. But real comedy places its individuals in a relation to the world which is complicated in a thousand ways, it places everything in relation to everything, and thus everything in an ironic relation. The war which has overwhelmed us all, and which today we have still not escaped and perhaps twenty years hence will not have escaped, functions like this. It places everything in a relation to everything, the apparently great to the apparently small, one set of conditions to a new set which stipulates the former again, the heroic to the mechanical, the pathetic to the financial and thus without end. First of all, when the war broke out, the hero was treated ironically: he became a

sapper who, instead of standing upright and fighting, burrowed
in the ground with his shovel; simultaneously, the individual
was being treated ironically to the extent that a feeling for
himself was destroyed by one for the masses; not only the
individual but indeed also the organized masses – the battalion,
the regiment, the army corps – were treated ironically by the
increasingly large and formless masses; then, however, even the
fighting masses – that frightening, wretched monster – were
treated ironically by something they felt themselves to be gov-
erned by, pushed on by, and for which it is difficult to find a
name: let us call it the spirit of the nations. But the moment
came when these formidable masses, which symbolized a unity,
were themselves treated ironically by the momentary omnipotence of single individuals who somehow had their hands on
the levers and the screws by which this clumsy whole could be
directed, if only for a moment. However, in this very moment
the conflicting currents of the mightiest and most debilitating
irony arose, the irony of the contrast between the grand ideal
solutions – which everyone was encouraged to talk about – and
the confusion of obstinate realities with which everyone had to
struggle; the irony of the tool opposed to the hand which felt it
was directing the tool, the irony of details, grounded in reality in
a thousand ways, opposed to the rash and consciously mislead-
ing solution. And then the moment came when, within these
enormous totalities, the concept of the nation was treated ironically by the concept of social class. The moment of coal and the
coalminer arrived:[2] the whole campaign, built upon both the
apparently spiritual, behind which the material was hidden, and
the apparently material, in which the spiritual – what we call
European civilization – was imprisoned, was made ironic by a
single material, sunlight stored in a mineral form; and all social
classes and even the working class were again made ironic by a
certain division of this class: the coalminers, who have a relation
to this material upon which everything depends, a relation in
which again a terrible irony is inherent; for they are bound in a

relation to precisely that material which they directly control, a relation which is not unlike slavery. But in the struggle for the soul of the coalminer, who had suddenly become master of the situation, the social and national slogans took on the most extreme form of irony; indeed, since he was bound more than other workers to the land, even those greatest of super-powers, geography and history, whose mutual irony flares up at times throughout this episode, became ironic in the struggle for him. The situation finally became an inexhaustible source of irony so that in the conquered lands (that is, virtually half of Europe) money lost its value against goods, even the most modest, a piece of bread or a metre of linen; and thus one could buy nothing at all whereas once one would blindly pay anything for that demonic substance which could purchase everything; and thus people began to barter for wide stretches of land; and in conjunction with these changes the privilege of mental work completely disappeared so that a grammar-school headmaster is paid as much as a porter, a governmental secretary rather less than a chauffeur.

With all this we find ourselves totally in the element of comedy – or, even more, in an element of universal irony such as no comedy in the world has depicted, unless it be that of Aristophanes; and this comedy arose as well during a war most unhappy for the poet's native city, a war which sealed its fate.[3] It is quite clear, of course, that it is the defeated who are touched by this ironic power of events. Whoever survives to the bitter end has the bandages removed from his eyes, acquires a clear mind, and gets behind things, almost like a dead man.

The poets of a century ago were sensitive to all these things, quite naturally, for they had to live through the French Revolution and the Napoleonic period, just as we have had to live through the present crises. Thus they created a fundamental principle out of irony for their outlook on life and art and called it 'Romantic Irony'. They thought it wrong if someone sank too deeply into his sorrows, and they were of the opinion that one must know how to love an object completely and how to see even the ridiculous in this object. They required one to think of all of life as a 'beautiful, ingenious deception' and as a 'magnificent spectacle', and whoever experienced this differently failed to grasp the meaning of the universe. Once the great storm had passed it was a period like ours in which the bitter is mixed with the stale; but they attained such an inner freedom that today it might appear to us as a kind of inebriation. Today this condition is more comprehensible to us than it could have been to any intervening generation, and we read and contemplate with wonder the words they wrote in a fiery flourish of the pen on the starless arch of the sky: *For the Lord is the Spirit. But where the Spirit is Lord, there is freedom*.

The substitute for dreams

What people look for in the cinema, said the friend with whom I had raised the subject, is a substitute for dreams. They want to fill their fantasy with pictures, with powerful pictures which summarize the essence of life; these pictures are, so to speak, formed out of the inner self of the viewer and bewilder him. For such pictures take life away from him. (I'm speaking of people in towns and large industrial conurbations, not of the others, the peasants, the sailors, the woodsmen or the highlanders.) Their heads are not empty by nature but are made empty by the life society forces them to lead. Look at these agglomerations of coal-blackened industrial areas with nothing more than a paltry stretch of withered meadow grass between them, and of the children who grow up here not one in a thousand has ever seen an owl or a squirrel or a spring; look at our cities, these endless intersecting rows of houses; the houses look like one another, they have a small door and rows of identical windows with the shutters beneath; nothing speaks to the person who passes by or who looks for a house; the only thing that speaks is the number.

The same is true of the factory, the workroom, the machine, the office where one pays one's taxes or fills out one's forms: nothing sticks save the number. Look at the work-day: a couple of levers, always the same ones; the same hammer or swingle or ratchet or lathe; and back home again. The gas cooker, the iron oven, the tools and small machines one depends upon and which with practice one masters, so that whoever finally masters them over and over again becomes himself a machine, a tool among tools. In the face of all this, countless hundreds of thousands flee to the darkened room with the moving pictures. That these pictures are mute is yet another attraction; they are mute like dreams. And at the deepest level, without knowing it, these people fear language; they fear in language the tool of society. The lecture room lies next to the cinema, the assembly room is a street further on, but they don't have this authority. The entrance to the cinema draws people to itself with an authority like that of the brandy cupboard: and yet it is something different. Above the lecture room is written in gold letters 'Knowledge is Power', but the cinema cries out more loudly, it cries out with pictures. The power which knowledge imparts has something about it they distrust, something not completely convincing, something virtually suspect. They feel this leads only more deeply into the machinery and further away from life which their senses and a deeper mystery which lurks beneath the senses tell them is *real* life. Knowledge, culture, the perception of relationships, all this perhaps loosens the manacles they feel at their hands, loosens them perhaps, for the moment – seemingly – in order perhaps later to fasten them yet more tightly. All this leads perhaps finally to new bondage, to yet greater servitude. (I am not saying that they say this; but a voice in them says it very softly.) And during all of this their inner self will remain empty. (They also say this to themselves without saying it aloud.) The peculiar, insipid emptiness of reality, its barrenness (for which brandy is also a cure), its flimsy mental images hanging in emptiness: none of this is really cured by what the lecture room offers. And the slogans at the political meeting, the columns in the newspaper they see every day – here too there is nothing which can really alleviate the barrenness of existence. That language of the educated or half-educated, whether written or spoken, is something alien. It crimps the surface but does not arouse what slumbers beneath. There is something too algebraic about this language, every letter covers up a digit, the digit is the abbreviation of a reality, all this points from a distance at something, at power, at that power in which one participates; but all this is too indirect, the connections are too intangible, it does not really captivate the mind, it leads it nowhere. In fact all this leaves a despondency behind and again that feeling of being the powerless part of a machine; and they all know of another power, a real one, the only real one: the power of dreams. When they were children they were powerful creatures. There were dreams at night but they were not limited to the night: they were there by day as well, they were everywhere: a dark corner, a whiff of air, the face of an animal or the shuffle of feet sufficed to make their continuous presence palpable. There was the dark space behind the cellar steps, an old barrel in the courtyard half full of rainwater, and a crate of rubbish; there was the door to a storehouse, the door to the loft, the door to the neighbour's flat from which someone emerged and in front of which one anxiously ducked past; or there was a beautiful person who threw the sweet, indefinable fright of dawning desire deep into the quivering depths of the heart – and now it is again that crate with enchanting junk which grows visible: the cinema. Here everything which is otherwise concealed behind the cold, opaque façades of the endless rows of houses is accessible; all doors open – into the apartments of the rich, into the young girl's room, into the public rooms of hotels, into the hide-outs of the thief, into the workshops of the alchemist. It's like flying through the air with the devil Asmodeus who makes walls transparent and exposes all secrets.[4] But is this not the lulling of an agonizing and often deceptive curiosity; here, as in the case of the dreamer, a deeper urge is fulfilled: dreams are deeds. The unrestrained gazing combines involuntarily with a sweet self-deception. It is like having complete authority over the pictures which are made to serve as they rush madly by – a complete authority over the entire existence of things. The landscape – house and park, forest and port – which flutters over from behind the figures only adds a kind of stifling music to this – stirring up God only knows what sort of longing and arrogance in the dark region where no written or spoken word penetrates. But in the meantime a whole literature in tatters flies by on the film – no, a whole confusion of literature: the leftover forms of thousands of dramas, novels, detective stories; historical anecdotes, hallucinations of visionaries, adventure stories. But at the same time one sees people and transparent gestures; there are expressions and glances which stir the soul and call it forth. They live and suffer, struggle and slip by before the eyes of the dreamer; and the dreamer knows he is awake; he need leave nothing of himself outside; everything in him, down into the innermost recesses, stares at this flickering reel of life which endlessly turns. It is the whole man who yields to this spectacle; not a single dream from tenderest childhood escapes the flicker, because we never forget our dreams. Out of every one of them, even those which we lose upon awaking, something remains in us – a gentle but decisive colouring of the emotions; habits which, more than the habits of everyday living, are those of the whole man; and all the suppressed frenzies in which the strength and particularity of the individual are lived inwardly to the full. All this subterranean vegetation shudders sympathetically down to its deepest roots, while the eyes gather in thousands of pictures of life from the flickering film. Indeed this dark rooting-ground of life, this region where the individual ceases to be an individual, where words so seldom penetrate, even the words of a prayer or the stammering words of love – it shudders in sympathy. From it, however, emerge the deepest and most secret feelings for life: the intuition of indestructibility, the belief in necessity and the contempt of that bare reality which is there only by accident. Once it is activated, the power we call mythic creation emerges from it. A symbol suddenly arises before this darkened glance out of the depths of being: the sensuous image of spiritual truth which is inaccessible to reason.

I know, my friend concluded, that there are very many ways of looking at these things. And I realize that from another standpoint they may be considered legitimate and nothing more than a product of a lamentable confusion of industrial greed, technological omnipotence, spiritual degradation and a crude curiosity which entices in every direction. To me, however, the atmosphere of the cinema seems to be the only atmosphere in which the people of our age – those who constitute the masses – participate in a horrible, at the same time meticulously prepared, spiritual inheritance; they enter into a purely immediate, completely unrestrained relation, life to life; and the cluttered, half-darkened room with the pictures whizzing by is to me – I can say it in no other way – almost sacred, like a place where souls, possessed by an obscure urge for self-preservation, take refuge and flee from the digit to the vision.

Beautiful language

'I love this language', someone wrote to me, 'already because of its formal beauty: the same pleasure which sends me back to these books also leads me back to the Latin prose of the German humanists. If I know few delights which can be compared to the exquisiteness of von Hutten's Latin dialogues,[5] it is because I have a greater regard for the form than for the content. Only the Germans could have made possible the expression *content is superior to form*. Language, in itself and purposeless, should and can be the object and the expression of an art. Here it is a matter of a feeling for form which for the Greeks and Romans was something simply self-evident.'

Certainly all this is quite correct and one may say that it points
to something more or less true, but one should take the matter a
bit further so as to get at the real truth. For 'beautiful' is a word
readily used, a word used without much reflection, and 'beautiful language' or 'beautifully written' is really a phrase used when
one has little else to say, one prompted when a book or a piece of
prose has said nothing. And yet no content is beautiful or
meaningful without a truly beautiful presentation, for content
first comes into the world through presentation, and a beautiful
book without beautiful language is as impossible as a beautiful
picture without beautiful painting; and this is precisely the
criterion of the beautifully written book – it means much to us,
unlike the poorly written book which means little or nothing,
though it may communicate something to us, or make us understand something, or illustrate the facts of a case for us. The
theologist or the anthroposophist, should he expound to us what
he reckons to be the most important insight or unwordly perception – and what higher subject could be imagined than the
relationship of the human and the divine? – should he expound
it like a salesman, or use the tired language of the newspaper, or
a feeble, stammering metaphorical language, he will not succeed. By contrast, Boccaccio wrote his tales in such a way that
everything there is prepared for eternity although they deal with
lovers' trysts, cuckoldry and other dirty tricks; but in their
imperishability and spiritual – one can say nothing other than
spiritual – charm, these frivolous tales stand next to Plato's
dialogues, whose content is the loftiest. Here one approaches
the notion that in itself there might be no lofty and no base
subject, but only reflections of the ineffable, universal
spiritual-sensuous principle in people, and these reflections
might be of a limitlessly varying degree and value, according
always to the nature of the mind which reflects. Our glance
moves suddenly from the subject back to the mouth which
speaks to us. And Montaigne's 'Tel par la bouche que sur le
papier'[6] is also a subtle truth which should not be underesti-

mated, for what accounts for the most profound magic of the beautifully written book is in fact quite certainly a kind of concealed oral quality, a kind of unveiling of the whole person through the language; but this oral quality assumes a listener; thus everything written is a dialogue and no simple expression. From this insight, a certain amount of light is cast, from an angle as it were, upon certain superior qualities by which we recognize the well-written book, the well-written page of prose – for it is prose, and by no means poetry, of which we are thinking and in which these qualities are usually emphasized: an agreeable idea or a meaningful, gritty conciseness, a charming or a deft way of drawing things together and passing on, pleasant cadences, a fine balance of the weight of what is presented and the weight of the presentation; the distance the author succeeds in creating in regard to his theme, the world in general and especially his reader, the constancy of contact with this listener in which the author is persistently felt. All these are expressions which point to a delicate, social relation between two people, and, to some extent, they apply to that spiritual-social principle of illumination which gives prose expression its astral body; and there is not one of them which could not be attributed equally well to the style of *Robinson Crusoe* or of Voltaire, to Lessing's[7] polemical writings or Søren Kierkegaard's[8] treatises. Upon contact with an ideal listener, the results amount to the same thing in all the styles. This listener is, so to speak, the representative of humanity and to have him participate in one's creation and to preserve the vital feeling of his presence is perhaps the finest, most powerful accomplishment which the creative energy of the prose writer has to realize. Because this listener must be imagined to be so sensitive, so quick to comprehend, so incorruptible in judgement, so capable of attentiveness, so one in head and heart, he seems almost to surpass the one who is speaking to him – and if it weren't so, it wouldn't be worth the effort of writing for him. And yet a certain imperfection must be attributed to him by the one who has created him, at least a certain imperfection in his development, above all the need of being shown many things; he must be given a powerful naïveté so that he can really be made to delight in what the book offers and thus experience something essentially new. Perhaps a whole hierarchy of books, especially out of those which instruct, could be established according to how sensitively and how meaningfully the relationship with the reader develops in them; and nothing would bring down a book and an author in this hierarchy more quickly than evidence that he had a muddled, inattentive and irreverent notion of this, his invisible client.

Thus there are always two – one who speaks or writes and one who listens or reads – and everything depends upon the contact between them; but the more meaningful it is, the loftier the regions it affects, the more the contact transfers weight to the giver, while the receiver, in these loftier regions, grows increasingly light and rare without ever, of course, ceasing to be there.

When Goethe says that whenever he opened up a page of Kant it seemed to him as if he had entered a bright room, he gives us an image of a mind full of light, communicating with the highest of all sources of light. But we detect – just as much as this gift for being like a light – other great spiritual talents in other writers: the strength which is inseparable from an inner order; the true self-respect which accompanies reverence; the rare glow of spiritual passion. We genuinely feel that we perceive the world in the productions of such a spirit – and indeed we perceive it not only in the objects he mentions but also in everything he leaves unmentioned but which is none the less included. This spirit has the power and mastery to pass over much of the overwhelming confusion of things – not forgetting about them, which would imply a weak and wandering mind, but passing them over with conscious deliberation; the unexpectedly established relations and, in turn, the syntheses, in which an attentiveness and a tension are suddenly revealed in all directions; finally even an apparent absentmindedness and arbitrariness, which at times can be enticing; all this belongs to the spiritual face of the writer, to the face we sense along with the reflection of the world as we read his prose. Like a tight-rope walker he passes before our eyes on a narrow rope stretched between church tower and church tower; the fear of the precipice into which he could fall at any moment does not appear to be there for him, and the gravity which insensibly pulls us all down appears powerless over his body. We follow his footsteps with rapture, higher and higher, as though he were leaving the earth altogether. He walks just as the pen of the good writer flies. Its movement, which enchants us and which is as singular as a human profile, is the balance of the walker who follows the rope unerringly through fears and the gravitational forces of a world; and a beautiful language is the revelation of an inner equilibrium, preserved under the most amazing conditions, in the midst of a multitude of intimidations, temptations and oppositions of all kinds.

Notes

1 Novalis was the pseudonym of Friedrich von Hardenberg (1772–1801), poet, philosopher and engineer. Some of the *Fragments* were published during his lifetime in *Blütenstaub* (*Pollen*, 1798) and *Glauben und Liebe* (*Faith and Love*, 1798).

2 After the fall of the Austro-Hungarian Empire in 1918, coal supplies to the new Austrian republic were withheld by the new Czechoslovak state as a gesture of independence and strength. The worst effects of the coal blockade were felt in late 1918 and early 1919. Demand for increased domestic production gave the Austrian miners the power to which Hofmannsthal refers.

3 The Athenian dramatist Aristophanes (*c*. 450– *c*. 388 BC) spent two-thirds of his life in the shadow of the Peloponnesian War. A pacifist, he used the theatre to show the folly of the war, e.g. in *The Acharnians* (425 BC).

4 Asmodeus was the devil of the sensuality in *Tobias*. The

Spanish novelist Vélez de Guevara (1579–1644) in *El diablo Cojuelo* (1641) – imitated later by Le Sage in *Le Diable boiteux* (1707) – gave the name to his principal character, a devil who lifts the roofs off houses in Madrid so as to reveal to whomever accompanies him the secrets within.

5 Ulrich von Hutten (1488–1523), a soldier, humanist, poet and prose writer, and poet laureate to Maximilian I in Augsburg, wrote *Conversations* in the manner of Lucian.

6 Michel de Montaigne (1533–92); 'Tel par la bouche que sur le papier' means literally 'As by mouth so on paper'. Montaigne's actual words go: 'Le parler que j'ayme, c'est un parler simple et naïf, tel sur le papier qu'à la bouche; un parler succulent et nerveux, court et serré.' ('The language I like is a simple, straightforward language written as it is spoken, a succulent and sinewy, brief and condensed language.')

7 Gotthold Ephraim Lessing (1729–81), the German playwright and critic.

8 Søren Kierkegaard (1813–55), the Danish theologian and philosopher.

Rainer Maria Rilke

Rainer Maria Rilke (1875–1926) was born in Prague and was intended for the military by his army-officer father and ultra-religious mother: he always regretted his purloined childhood. Largely self-taught, he read philosophy, art history, law and literature at Prague University and produced two unexceptional books of verse. He went to Munich in 1896, then to Berlin, beginning a lifelong friendship with Lou Andreas Salomé whom he accompanied to Russia in 1899 and 1900. After marrying the sculptress Clara Westhoff in 1901 he settled in Worpswede near Bremen. In 1902 he left for Paris to write about Rodin whom he served for a while as a secretary. He was based in Paris until the War, supported by aristocratic admirers. Moving to Switzerland in 1919 he settled in 1921 in a small stone tower, the Château de Muzot, his base until his death.

WRITINGS

These include *Das Stundenbuch* (*The Book of Hours*, 1905); *Das Buch der Bilder* (*The Book of Images*, 1906); *Neue Gedichte* (*New Poems*, 1907 and 1908); a sombre, dense prose work, *The Notebooks of Malte Laurids Brigge* (1910); his crowning statements were published in 1923, *Sonette an Orpheus* (*Sonnets to Orpheus*) and *Duineser Elegien* (*Duino Elegies*, written 1912–22). His correspondence is enchanting and prolific, nearly thirty volumes now having been published.

'Auguste Rodin: Second Part (Extract)'. 'Rodin: First Part' was written in 1902 as an introduction to the sculptor's work for the German public. 'Rodin: Second Part' is a lecture first written in 1905 and revised in 1907 to accompany the first part in a new edition.

'The Letter of the Young Worker', first published posthumously in 1933, was written in February 1922, the miraculous month when the *Sonnets* were written and the *Elegies* completed. It proceeds from prose notes of a memoir on the Belgian poet Émile Verhaeren (see p. 11, n. 8), the 'Herr V.' here.

AUGUSTE RODIN: SECOND PART (EXTRACT)

There are several great names which, if spoken aloud just now, would create a friendship between us, and, with it, a sense of warmth and unity, so that I – only apparently separate from you – would be speaking as though in your midst: through you like one of your voices. The name which stands far away like a constellation of five great stars over this evening cannot yet be spoken aloud. It would trouble you, would excite you, would arouse sympathy or resistance – whereas now I need your silence and want to leave the surface of your receptiveness undisturbed.

I would ask those who can to forget the name in question, and I am asking everyone to forget even more. You are accustomed to hearing speakers talk about art, and who would want to conceal the fact that such words enjoy your favour? A certain beautiful and powerful movement which can no longer be hidden has, like the flight of a great bird, attracted your gaze: but now you are being asked to lower your eyes during the course of the evening. For it is not my desire to direct your attention out there, into the skies of uncertain developments, nor to make predictions about modern art and its bird-like flight.

I feel like someone who must ask you to recall your childhood, not only yours, but all that ever was childhood. The important thing is to awaken memories in you which are not your own, which are older than you; relationships should be restored and connections renewed, though they may now be distant from you.

If my purpose were to speak to you about people, I could start where you just now left off as you came in; breaking into your conversation, as though of my own accord, I would have pronounced on everything – wrenched up and carried along by this troubled age on whose shores all things human seem to lie, soaked by it and, in an unexpected way, reflected in it. But in attempting to get a grasp on the problem, it becomes clear to me that I should speak to you not about people but about things.

Things

In pronouncing that word (do you hear it?) a silence is created – the silence which surrounds things. All movement ceases, becomes contour, and out of past and future time something enduring is sealed off: the space, the calm of things compelled to do nothing. But no: you do not yet feel the silence which is created this way. The word *things* passes you by, it means nothing to you: it means too much and thus you feel indifferent. So now I am glad I called up childhood; perhaps it can help me to endear you to this word which is associated with many memories.

If you can, look back with your no longer accustomed, adult feelings to one of those children's things you spent a lot of time with. Do you recall if there was anything closer, more trusted and necessary than such a thing; if not everything – except it – was capable of making you feel hurt, of startling you with a pain or confusing you with a doubt? If there was kindness in your first experiences and trust and no loneliness – isn't it to be thanked for all this? Was it not with this thing that you first shared your little heart, like a piece of bread which had to suffice for two?

Later, in the legends of the saints, you found a devout joyousness, a blissful humility, a preparedness to be everything you could imagine, because a little piece of wood had once done all this for you, had accepted and borne it all. This small, forgotten object which was prepared to mean everything brought you into confidence with a thousand things, because it played a thousand roles, was animal and tree and king and child – and when it withdrew, everything was there. This something, valueless as it was, prepared your relations with the world; it led you to events and to people and even more: you experienced in it, in its being, in its 'looking more or less like this', in its final destruction or its puzzling disappearance, everything human and even the mystery of death.

You can barely recall this any more and you are seldom conscious of the fact that you still need things like those from childhood which ask for your trust, your love and your devotion. How do these things come to be as they are? How are things generally related to us? What is their history?

Very early on one formed things, with difficulty, following the model of the natural things one came across; one made tools and vessels, and it must have been a remarkable experience to see what one had made oneself accepted as equal with and as real as what *was*. Then something arose, blindly, out of furious labour, carrying traces of a threatened, exposed life; it was still warm with life, and though hardly completed and put away, it was assimilated with other things; it assumed their composure, their silent dignity, only it looked over as if filled with the melancholy understanding of the grief it caused. This experience was so powerful and unusual that one understands how much created things owe their origin to it. Thus perhaps the most ancient images of gods drew on this experience and were attempts to form, with the human and animal elements around one, something that did not perish with them, something enduring, something raised to a higher level: a thing.

What sort of a thing? A beautiful one? No. Who would have known what beauty is? An imitative one. A thing in which one recognized what one loved and what one feared and what, in all of this, was incomprehensible.

Do you recall such things? Perhaps there's one you considered to be quite trifling for a long while – but then one day you noticed its imploring glance, that special, almost desperate earnestness which they all have; and then, didn't you notice how a beauty came over this image, almost against its will, a beauty you didn't believe possible?

If there ever was such a moment I want to appeal to it now. It is that very moment which enables things to re-enter your life. For not one of them can stir you if you do not allow it to astonish you with that beauty which is impossible to overlook. Beauty is always something that has been added, and we don't know what.

That an aesthetic view existed which claimed to explain beauty confused you; this view also brought out artists who felt their task to be the creation of beauty. And indeed it has not yet become superfluous to repeat that one cannot 'make' beauty. No one has ever 'made' beauty. One can only create friendly or sublime conditions for that which may sometimes linger with us: an altar and fruit and a flame – the making itself is not in our power. And the thing itself which, irrepressibly, proceeds from the hands of a man is like the Eros of Socrates,[1] is a daemon, is between God and man, not beautiful itself, but a pure love of beauty and a pure longing for it.

Now imagine how this insight must – should the creator have it – change everything. The artist guided by this knowledge need not think of beauty; he knows just as little as anyone else about its nature. Guided by the urge to find uses which exceed those of the thing, he only knows about the conditions under which these uses may be made of the thing. And his calling is to become familiar with these conditions and to acquire the ability to produce them.

But whoever studies these conditions attentively and exhaustively discovers that they do not go beyond the surface and go nowhere into the interior of the thing; and that the only thing man can do is to produce a surface sealed in a specific way, nowhere accidental, a surface which, like that of natural things, is surrounded by atmosphere, is shaded and illuminated – only a surface – otherwise nothing. Compared to all the lofty, pretentious and capricious words used to evoke it, art seems suddenly confined to small and sober quarters, to banality, to the handiwork of an artisan. For what does it mean to make a surface?

But let us think about this for a moment: is not everything that surrounds us, that we perceive and represent and give a meaning to, a surface? And what we call spirit and soul and love: is not all this a gentle alteration of the small surface of a face nearby? And must not anyone who wants to give us something formed restrict himself to what corresponds tangibly to his means, restrict himself to the form which he can hold and explore? And whoever is able to see and give form, would he not (almost without knowing it) give us everything that is spiritual as well – all that was ever called longing or pain or bliss or that, in its ineffable spirituality, can have no name at all?

For every joy that stirred a heart, every greatness which intimidated contemplation itself, every single distant, changing thought were at one time nothing but pursed lips, knitted brows or curling shadows on a forehead; and this straining at the mouth, that line above the eyebrows, this darkness upon a face – perhaps they were there exactly like this before: as the drawing of an animal, as the ridge of a crag, as a dimple on a fruit. . . .

There is but one single surface, moved and modified in a thousand ways. One was able to imagine the whole world for a moment in this idea, and the world became simple – was put in the hands like a task for the person who had this thought. For whether something can take on life depends not upon great ideas but upon whether one can fashion a handiwork for oneself out of them, something for everyday use, something which will stand by one to the very end. . . .

Note

1 Socrates (470–399 BC) expounds on Eros or Love in Plato's
   Symposium, where he says that Love is the soul's reaching out
   for a good it does not possess, manifest in a low form in the
   desire to procreate and the good of immortality. The highest
   form, Socrates suggests, is the longing for unity with supreme
   beauty.

THE LETTER OF THE YOUNG WORKER

Some of your poems were read to us at a gathering last Thurs-
day, Herr V., and, wishing to inquire further and knowing no
better way, I thought I would write to you about what is on my
mind, in so far as I am able.

The day after that reading I went by chance to a Christian
meeting, and perhaps that was what really provided the shock
which got me excited and aroused such movement and activity
in me that I turn now to you with all my energies. To start
anything requires an enormous effort. I can't *start*. I'm simply
jumping over what should have been the beginning. Nothing is
so strong as silence. If each one of us were not born into the
midst of speech, silence would never have been interrupted.

Herr V., I'm not speaking about the evening when we were
listening to your poetry. I'm speaking of the other one. I'm
forced to say: who indeed – I can't express it any other way, *who*
is this Christ who gets mixed up in everything, who has known
nothing about us, about our work, about our misery, nothing
about our happiness, such as we carry it out, endure it and
summon it up – in our own times – and who, in spite of this, it
seems, demands time and again to be the *first* person in our life?
Or has someone put these words in his mouth? What does he
want of us? They say he wants to help us. Yes, but he has little
advice to offer when near us. The circumstances in his times

were completely different. Or if it's not a question of circumstances, suppose he were to walk right in, here in my room or
over there in the factory – would everything suddenly be different and better? Would my heart open up in me and, so to speak,
extend on another plane out to him? My feelings tell me that he
cannot come, that there would be no sense in it. Not only is our
world outwardly different – it has no entrance for him either. He
wouldn't be *visible* in a ready-made coat, that's quite right, he
wouldn't be visible. It's no accident that he went about in a robe
without seams,[1] and I believe that the core of light in him which
made him shine so brightly,[2] day and night, has long been
dispersed and distributed differently. But if he were so great –
and I feel that this would be the least we could ask of him – he
should somehow have been burnt up, leaving no remains
behind, no remains at all – not a trace. . . .

I can't imagine how the *cross*, which was really only a crossroads, can *endure*. Surely it shouldn't be stamped on us everywhere like a brandmark. It should have disappeared with him.
For isn't it true that he simply wanted to create the higher tree
on which we could ripen better? On the cross he is this new tree
in God, and we should be warm, happy fruit up there on it.

One shouldn't rattle on about what *once* was, rather one
should think that the *afterwards* began at this very moment.
This tree, it seems to me, should have become so much one with
us, or we with it, *on* it, that we shouldn't give it a second
thought, rather we should simply think of God, whose intention
it was, none the less, to hold us up all the more purely.

When I say God, that's an important conviction in me I never
learned. I imagine the whole of creation saying this word without a thought, though often with deep reflection. If Christ has
helped us to say it fully and more genuinely, with a clearer voice,
so much the better, but let's leave him out of the matter once and
for all. Let's not force ourselves to retreat to the toil and misery
it cost him in order to 'save' us, as they say. Give us this salvation
at last. Here the Old Testament would be relevant, filled, as it is,

with fingers pointing to God; and here, when the going is hard, you always fall down in the midst of God. Once I tried to read the Koran. I didn't get very far but I understood enough to know that again here that powerful finger is pointing and that at the end of the direction which it indicates God is standing, caught in His eternal ascent, in an East which will never be exhausted. Christ certainly wanted the same. To point. But people have behaved like dogs here, not understanding what a pointing finger is, thinking they should snap at it. Instead of going on from the crossroads where a signpost was erected in the night of sacrifice, instead of leaving the crossroads behind, Christianity set up camp here and claimed to live in Christ, although there was no room in him, not for his mother, not for Mary Magdalen; and this is true of anyone who signals, for this is a gesture and not a lodging-place. And they don't dwell in Christ, these people with stubborn hearts who set him up again and again and live with the support of a slanting or completely overturned cross. Their conscience is crowded, there's a queue on an overfilled spot, and they are to blame that the journey follows the direction of the cross's arms no further. They've turned Christianity into a *métier*, a bourgeois profession, *sur place*, a pond alternately drained and filled. Everything they do themselves, following their irrepressible nature (in so far as they are still alive), contradicts this remarkable pose, and so they muddy their own waters and have to replenish them again and again. They are all too eager to make the here and now – which we should desire and trust – evil and worthless; and so, more and more, they surrender the earth to those ready to extract at least a temporary, immediately profitable advantage out of it – this relinquished, distrusted earth, fit, as they see it, for little else. Isn't this increasing exploitation of life the consequence of centuries which have devalued the here-and-now? What madness it is to send us off chasing a beyond when we are surrounded here by problems and expectations and futures. What fraud to steal images of the joys of the here-and-now in order to hawk them behind our backs to heaven! Oh, it's high time the impoverished earth reclaimed all those loans made from earthly joys to provide for what lies beyond the future. Does death really grow more transparent as a result of these fountains of light we've slipped behind it? And isn't everything which is taken away from here – since voids exist to be filled – replaced by deception; isn't that why cities are full of so much ugly artificial light and noise, because true radiance and song have been surrendered to a Jerusalem which will be entered only later? Christ may have been right when, in an age of dissipated and unrespected gods, he demeaned earthly things, although (I can't imagine it otherwise) it amounts to an affront to God not to see in what has been granted and conceded to us – if only we could use it properly – something that could make us joyful to the limits of our senses! The right use, that's the point. To take the here-and-now in our hands, so to speak, earnestly, lovingly, awfully, as our one and only possession for the time being: to put it crudely, it's like the 'directions for the use of God' which Francis of Assisi wanted to write down in his song to the sun,[3] which was more magnificent to him as he lay dying than the cross whose only purpose was to *point* to the sun. But what we call the church grew in the meantime into such a confusion of voices that the dying man's song, everywhere outsounded, was preserved only by a few simple monks and was endlessly echoed by the countryside of his charming valley. How often such attempts must have been made to bring about a reconciliation of Christian renunciation and the obvious friendliness and cheerfulness of the earth! Yet within the church none the less, indeed in its own head, the here-and-now was given its due and allowed its inborn richness. Why isn't the church celebrated for being sturdy enough not to collapse under the weight of the lives of certain popes whose thrones were loaded with bastards, courtesans and murdered men? Was there not more Christianity in them than in the dour reinstators of the gospels – namely, something living, incessant, and protean? Of course we don't know *what* the results of the great teachings will be, we must only let them flow unhindered and not be frightened should they suddenly plunge into the divided nature of life and roll under the earth in unrecognizable streams.

Once I worked for a couple of months in Marseille. It was a special period for me and I owe much to it. By chance I came across a young painter who remained my friend until his death. He suffered from lung trouble and at the time had just returned from Tunis. We were together a lot and as the end of my job coincided with his return to Paris we arranged to stop several days in Avignon. These remain unforgettable for me. Partly because of the city itself, its buildings and their surroundings, and also because of a curiously intense intimacy during this time, my friend talked to me about many things, especially about his *inner* life, with an eloquence that seems characteristic of such sick people at times. Everything he said had a peculiar, prophetic force; through everything which surfaced in the almost breathless conversations you could more or less see the bottom, the stones on the bottom. . . . I mean by that something more than what is merely our own: I mean nature itself, its oldest and solidest aspect which we none the less touch in so many places and upon which we probably depend in our most excited moments, since its slope determines our bearing. An experience of love, unexpected and happy, was added to this; his heart was held unusually high for days and the light of his life shot up to a considerable height. To view an exceptional town and a more than pleasing landscape with someone in such a mood is a rare privilege; and thus, when I think back about it, those equally tender and passionate spring days also appear to me as the only holidays I have known in my life. The period was so ridiculously short, for someone else it would have sufficed only for a few impressions; to me, not being used to having time off, it seemed a great deal. In fact it's almost wrong to use the word *time* for what was really a new state of freeness, quite palpably a *space*, a feeling of being surrounded by openness, in which there is no transience. If such a thing can be said, I retrieved childhood and a bit of my former youthfulness which never had time to grow up in me naturally. I looked, I learned, I understood – and the experience whereby I came to say 'God' so easily, so truthfully, so – as my friend would have put it – effortlessly, came out of these days as well. How could this house, which the popes had built for themselves here,[4] not strike me with force? I had the impression that it couldn't possess any interior whatsoever, but that it must have been put together in layers of solid blocks as if the only concern of the excommunicated there was to pile up the weight of the papacy, its excessive weight, on the scales of history. And this church palace truthfully towers up above the antique torso of a statue of Hercules which has been embedded in the wall of the craggy foundation – 'Is it not as though', said Pierre, 'it grew up tremendously out of this single seed?' That *this* is Christianity, in one of its transformations, would make much more sense to me than any attempt to locate its strength and flavour in the weaker and weaker infusion of that *tisane* which they claim to have prepared from its first, most tender leaves.

Aren't the cathedrals the body of that spirit we are asked to think of as truly Christian? I could believe that a contorted statue of a Greek goddess slumbers in some of them; so much blossoming, so much existence has shot up through them – even if, when gripped by the fear of their times, they fled, so to speak, that concealed body and strove for the heavens which were supposed to be kept open by the ringing of their bells.

Since my return from Avignon I've often gone into churches, evenings and on Sunday – first alone . . . later. . . .

I have a sweetheart, almost still a child, who works at home so that when there's little work about she often gets in a bad way. She is capable, she could easily find a job in a factory, but she is afraid of the boss. Her idea of freedom is boundless. You will not be surprised to learn that she feels God to be such a boss, the 'Arch-boss' as she told me once, laughing, but with such fright

in her eyes. It took her a long while to decide to accompany me
one evening to St Eustache where I enjoy going because of the
May devotions. Once we went off to Maux together and looked
at the gravestones in the church there. Gradually she noticed
that God leaves you in peace in the churches, that he demands
nothing; one might think he wasn't there at all – but, Marthe
said, in the moment you feel like saying he isn't in the church
either, something holds you back. Perhaps it's only what the
people themselves over the centuries have introduced into this
noble, strangely powerful air. Perhaps it's only that the vi-
bration of the sweet and mighty music never quite escapes; in
fact it must have permeated the stones long ago and they must be
remarkably excited ones, those which form these pillars and
arches; and if the stones are hard and difficult to penetrate, the
repeated singing, the assaults of the organ, the storms of song
every Sunday and the hurricanes of the great holidays finally
affect them. Doldrums – that's exactly what prevails in the old
churches. I said it to Marthe. Doldrums. We listened, she
understood it immediately, she has a marvellously receptive
character. Since then we have often gone in here and there when
we heard singing, and would stand close to one another. The
most beautiful is when we stand before a glass window, one of
those old picture windows with lots of sections, each filled with
figures, large people and small towers and all kinds of goings-
on. Nothing was too strange for them, you see castles and battles
and a hunt, and the fine, white stag appears again and again in
the bright red and burning blue. Once I was given some very old
wine to drink. These windows are the same to the eyes, except
that the wine was only dark red in the mouth – but this here is
the same in blue and violet and green. There is absolutely
everything in the old churches, no aversion to anything, whereas
in the modern ones only those windows which preach good
examples are to be seen. Here one sees the wicked and the evil
and the terrible; the deformed, the distressed, the ugly, the
unjust, and one is supposed to understand that all this is loved

somehow for God's sake. Here is the angel, which doesn't exist, and the devil, which doesn't exist either; and man, who does exist, is between them, and I can't help myself saying that their unreality makes him more real for me. In this sense I can understand better the man pictured here than the one in the street, among people who have nothing recognizable at all about them. But this is difficult to express. And what I want to say now is even more difficult. As far as the 'boss' or his power is concerned (this also became clear to me in there when we gave ourselves completely over to the music), there is only *one* remedy for it: to go further than it goes itself. By that I mean: one should make an effort to see in every power that makes a claim upon us *all* power, the whole of power, power itself, God's power. One should say to oneself, there is only *one* power, and understand the trifling, false, defective ones as standing for the one which lays a rightful claim upon us. Wouldn't it be harmless in this way? If one always saw power itself in every power, even in wicked and evil ones, that is, in *whatever* finally claims the right to be powerful, wouldn't one surmount unscathed, so to speak, both arbitrary and despotic forces? Isn't this precisely our relationship with all great unknown forces? We experience none in their purity. On the contrary, we experience each with all its deficiencies (which have perhaps exactly the same proportions as our own deficiencies). With all learned men, with discoverers and inventors, has not the assumption that they were dealing with the great forces suddenly led to the greatest? I am young and there is a lot of rebellion in me; I can't be sure of acting judiciously in every case when impatience and disgust get the better of me, but deep inside I know that submission leads further than rebellion; it makes domination difficult and contributes indescribably to the glorification of true power. The rebel runs away from the attraction of a centre of power and he might succeed in eluding its gravitational field; but beyond this he stands in a void and must look around for another gravitational force to draw him in. And this one will usually be even less legitimate than the first. Therefore, why not see straight away the greatest power in whatever affects us, undistracted by its weaknesses and fluctuations? Unbridled will naturally collides with law at some point and we save energy if we allow it to develop of its own accord. True, this is part of a slow and lengthy process which is so much at odds with the furious busy-ness of our age. But next to the fastest movements there will always be slow ones, of such extreme slowness that we can't even experience their passing. But isn't mankind's duty to attend to what lies beyond the powers of individuals? From its point of view, what is slow is often fastest, that is, it turns out that we called it slow because it was something immeasurable.

It seems to me that there is something completely immeasurable which men never tire of miscalculating, with their scales, measurements and adjustments. And here in that love which, with an unbearable mixture of contempt, eagerness and curiosity they call 'sensual', here are found for certain the worst effects of that degradation which Christianity felt bound to inflict on the earthly. Everything is distortion and repression, though we proceed from this most profound event recognizing in it none the less the centre of our delights. It's increasingly incomprehensible for me how a doctrine, which says we do wrong precisely where all living creatures enjoy their most blessed right, is allowed to propagate itself with such singlemindedness when it never has proven its value.

Here I think again of the lively conversations I had with my late friend in the meadows of the Barthelasse Island, in the spring and later on. Even in the night before his death (he died the following afternoon shortly after five o'clock) he opened up such pure vistas for me into a realm of blindest suffering that my life seemed to begin anew for me in a thousand places and, when I wanted to answer, I had no voice. I didn't know that there were such things as tears of joy. I cried my first, like a beginner, in the hands of the man who was to die the next day and felt how life's torrent rose in Pierre again and overflowed, when these hot tears were added. Am I getting carried away? But of course I'm talking now about something *excessive*.

Why, I ask you, Herr V., if people want to help us, we who are often so helpless, why do they leave us in the lurch at the roots of all experience? Whoever comes to our help *there* could be sure that we would require nothing else of him, since the help he would send down to us would have grown of itself out of our life, and would have increased and strengthened simultaneously with it. And it would never cease. What don't they insinuate into our most secret possession? How we have to prowl around it in order to sneak in like burglars and thieves, into our own fine sex in which we wander about and collide and stumble, so to speak, till we rush out again like detected criminals, into the twilight of Christianity. If guilt or sin had to be invented because of the inner tension of our soul, why wasn't it associated with another part of our body, why was it allowed to end up where it is in the hope that it would dissolve into our pure fountain, poison and dirty it? Why has sex been made homeless instead of being celebrated as our natural right?

Very well, I will admit that it shouldn't belong to us who can't control and be responsible for such inexhaustible bliss. But why don't we belong to God at *that* very point?

There is marriage, a churchman would tell me, although he couldn't fail to ignore how things fare with that institution. It's no use trying to reconcile the urge to reproduce with the notion of grace – sex isn't there for posterity alone, it is the secret of my own life. And many people have pushed sex to one side, apparently only so that it shouldn't occupy a central place – and in the process they lose their balance. What good does it do! The awful falsehood and uncertainty of our age is founded upon the denied joy of sex, upon this strange, distorted prohibition which constantly grows more powerful, separating us from the rest of nature, and even from the child, although, as I found out that unforgettable night, the child's innocence lies in no way with its having no sex, so to speak – 'on the contrary,' Pierre said with

almost no expression, 'that inconceivable joy, which for us
awakes in *one* spot in the fruit flesh of the closed embrace, is
imperceptibly distributed throughout the child's whole body.'
In order to describe our present state of sensuality one would
have to say: we were once child *all over*, now we are a child in
only one spot. If any of us are certain of this and can give
evidence – why do we allow one generation after the other to
grow up in the ruins of Christian prejudices and to behave like
mannequins in a shop window, stock-still in the narrowest of
spaces, between a pair of renunciations!?

Herr V., I write and write. Almost a whole night has gone by.
I must pull myself together. Have I said that I work in a factory?
I work in the office and often with a machine. Earlier I was able
to study for a short time. Now, let me just say how I feel. You
see, I want to be of use to God, just as I am; what I do here, the
work, I want to continue with it in His direction, without having
the fountain of my water interrupted, if I may put it like that –
not by Christ, who was once the water for many. The machine,
for example, I couldn't explain that to him, he doesn't understand. I know you aren't laughing; if I put it so awkwardly, it's
probably best this way. God, on the other hand, I feel I can bring
it to *Him*, my machine and its first fruits or indeed all my labours
will go straight to Him, unhindered: just as once it was easy for
the shepherds to bring a lamb or the fruit of the field or the finest
grapes to the gods of their lives.

You see, Herr V., I was able to write this long letter without
having need of the word belief – not once. That seems to me to
be a complicated and ceremonious affair, not mine. I don't want
to be evil for Christ's sake but good for God's sake. I don't want
to be considered a sinner from the outset, perhaps I'm not one.
My mornings are so pure that I could speak with God – I need no
one to help me write letters to Him.

I only know your poems from that reading the other evening.
I own few books, mostly about my job. A couple of course about
art and history which I discovered myself. But those poems, you

will agree, have moved me quite a bit. My friend once said: 'Give us teachers who celebrate the here-and-now for us.' You *are* one of these.

Notes

1 'When the soldiers had crucified Jesus they took his garments and made four parts, one for each soldier; also his tunic. But the tunic was without seam, woven from top to bottom' (John 19:23).
2 'And after six days Jesus took with him Peter and James and John his brother, and led them up a high mountain apart. And he was transfigured before them, and his face shone like the sun, and his garments became white as light' (Matthew 17:1-2).
3 Saint Francis of Assisi (1181/2–1226) refers in his *Canticle of Creatures* (also called *Canticle of the Sun*) to all of nature as his brother or sister, Sister Moon, Brother Sun, etc.
4 The Palace of the Popes, a fortress palace in a civic Gothic style begun by John XXII in Avignon, the papal seat from 1305 to 1377.

Wallace Stevens

Wallace Stevens (1879–1955) was born and reared in German Pennsylvania, the son of 'a lawyer, a Presbyterian and a Democrat'. He studied at Harvard University where he met the philosopher George Santayana, an abiding influence. After working briefly as a reporter for the New York Herald Tribune, *he read law at the New York Law School and was called to the bar. His earnest efforts in poetry were encouraged by publication in* Poetry: A Magazine of Verse *(1914). He joined the legal office of the Hartford Accident and Indemnity Company (1916) and resided in Hartford, Connecticut for the rest of his life. Elevated to vice-president of the same firm (1934), he was said to have been 'an outstanding attorney in the bond claim field'.*

WRITINGS

The first volume of poetry appeared in his forty-third year, *Harmonium* (1923); this was followed by *Ideas of Order* (1936), *The Man with the Blue Guitar* (1937), *Parts of a World* (1942), *The Auroras of Autumn* (1950), *The Necessary Angel: Essays on Reality and the Imagination* (1951) and *Collected Poems* (1954).

'Imagination as Value' was read to the English Institute at Columbia University in 1948, and was included in *The Necessary Angel*.

IMAGINATION AS VALUE

It does not seem possible to say of the imagination that it has a certain single characteristic which of itself gives it a certain single value, as, for example, good or evil. To say such a thing would be the same thing as to say that the reason is good or evil or, for that matter, that human nature is good or evil. Since that is my first point, let us discuss it.

Pascal[1] called the imagination the mistress of the world. But as he seems never to have spoken well of it, it is certain that he did not use this phrase to speak well of it. He called it the deceptive element in man, the mistress of error and duplicity and yet not always that, since there would be an infallible measure of truth if there were an infallible measure of untruth. But being most often false, it gives no sign of its quality and indicates in the same way both the true and the false. A little farther on in his *Pensées* he speaks of magistrates, their red robes, their ermines in which they swathe themselves, like furry cats, the palaces in which they sit in judgment, the fleurs-de-lis, and the whole necessary, august apparatus. He says, and he enjoys his own malice in saying it, that if medical men did not have their cassocks and the mules they wore and if doctors did not have their square hats and robes four times too large, they would never have been able to dupe the world, which is incapable of resisting so genuine a display. He refers to soldiers and kings, of whom he speaks with complete caution and respect, saying that they establish themselves by force, the others 'par grimace'. He justifies monarchs by the strength they possess and says that it is necessary to have a well-defined reason to regard like anyone else the Grand Seigneur surrounded, in his superb seraglio, by forty thousand janissaries.

However this may be, if respect for magistrates can be established by their robes and ermines and if justice can be made to prevail by the appearance of the seats of justice and if vast populations can be brought to live peacefully in their homes and to lie down at night with a sense of security and to get up in the morning confident that the great machine of organized society is ready to carry them on, merely by dressing a few men in uniform and sending them out to patrol the streets, the sort of thing that was the object of Pascal's ridicule and that was, to his way of thinking, an evil, or something of an evil, becomes to our way of thinking a potent good. The truth is, of course, that we do not really control vast populations in this way. Pascal knew perfectly well that the chancellor had force behind him. If he felt in his day that medicine was an imaginary science, he would not feel so today. After all, Pascal's understanding of the imagination was a part of his understanding of everything else. As he lay dying, he experienced a violent convulsion. His sister, who attended him, described the scene. He had repeatedly asked that he might receive communion. His sister wrote:

> God, who wished to reward a desire so fervent and so just, suspended this convulsion as by a miracle and restored his judgment completely as in the perfection of his health, in a manner that the parish priest, entering into his room with the sacrament, cried to him: 'Here is he whom you have so much desired.' These words completely roused him and as the priest approached to give him communion, he made an effort, he raised himself half way without help to receive it with more respect; and the priest having interrogated him, following the custom, on the principal mysteries of the faith, he responded distinctly: 'Yes, monsieur, I believe all that with all my heart.' Then he received the sacred wafer and extreme unction with feelings so tender that he poured out tears. He replied to everything, thanked the priest and as the priest blessed him with the holy ciborium, he said, 'Let God never forsake me.'

Thus, in the very act of dying, he clung to what he himself had called the delusive faculty. When I said a moment ago that he had never spoken well of it, I did not overlook the fact that 'this superb power, the enemy of reason', to use his own words, did not, and could not, always seem the same to him. In a moment of indifference, he said that the imagination disposes all things and that it is the imagination that creates beauty, justice and happiness. In these various ways, the example of Pascal demonstrates how the good of the imagination may be evil and its evil good. The imagination is the power of the mind over the possibilities of things; but if this constitutes a certain single characteristic, it is the source not of a certain single value but of as many values as reside in the possibilities of things.

A second difficulty about value is the difference between the imagination as metaphysics and as a power of the mind over external objects, that is to say, reality. Ernst Cassirer[2] in his *An Essay on Man* says:

> In romantic thought the theory of poetic imagination had reached its climax. Imagination is no longer that special human activity which builds up the human world of art. It now has universal metaphysical value. Poetic imagination is the only clue to reality. Fichte's idealism is based upon his conception of 'productive imagination'. Schelling declared in his *System of Transcendental Idealism* that art is the consummation of philosophy. In nature, in morality, in history we are still living in the propylaeum of philosophical wisdom; in art we enter into the sanctuary itself. The true poem is not the work of the individual artist; it is the universe itself, the one work of art which is forever perfecting itself.

Professor Cassirer speaks of this as 'exuberant and ecstatic praise of poetic imagination'. In addition, it is the language of what he calls 'romantic thought' and by romantic thought he means metaphysics. When I speak of the power of the mind over external objects I have in mind, as external objects, works of art as, for example, the sculptures of Michelangelo with what Walter Pater[3] calls 'their wonderful strength verging, as in the things of the imagination great strength always does, on what is singular or strange', or, in architecture, the formidable public buildings of the British or the architecture and decoration of churches, as, say, in the case of the Jesuit church at Lucerne, where one might so easily pass from the real to the visionary without consciousness of change. Imagination, as metaphysics, leads us in one direction and, as art, in another.

When we consider the imagination as metaphysics, we realize that it is in the nature of the imagination itself that we should be quick to accept it as the only clue to reality. But alas! we are no sooner so disposed than we encounter the logical positivists. In *Language, Truth and Logic*, Professor Ayer[4] says that

> it is fashionable to speak of the metaphysician as a kind of misplaced poet. As his statements have no literal meaning, they are not subject to any criteria of truth or falsehood; but they may still seem to express, or arouse, emotions, and thus be subject to ethical or aesthetic standards. And it is suggested that they may have considerable value, as means of moral inspiration, or even as works of art. In this way, an attempt is made to compensate the metaphysician for his extrusion from philosophy.

It appears from this that the imagination as metaphysics, from the point of view of the logical positivist, has at least seeming values. During the last few months, the *New Statesman* of London has been publishing letters growing out of a letter sent to it by a visitor to Oxford, who reported that Professor Ayer's book had 'acquired almost the status of a philosophic Bible'. This led Professor Joad[5] to look up the book and see for himself. He reported that the book teaches that

> If . . . God is a metaphysical term, if, that is to say, He belongs to a reality which transcends the world of sense-experience . . . to say that He exists is neither true nor false. This position . . . is neither atheist nor agnostic; it cuts deeper than either, by asserting that all talk about God, whether pro or anti, is twaddle.

What is true of one metaphysical term is true of all.

Then, too, before going on, we must somehow cleanse the imagination of the romantic. We feel, without being particularly intelligent about it, that the imagination as metaphysics will survive logical positivism unscathed. At the same time, we feel, and with the sharpest possible intelligence, that it is not worthy to survive if it is to be identified with the romantic. The imagination is one of the great human powers. The romantic belittles it. The imagination is the liberty of the mind. The romantic is a failure to make use of that liberty. It is to the imagination what sentimentality is to feeling. It is a failure of the imagination precisely as sentimentality is a failure of feeling. The imagination is the only genius. It is intrepid and eager and the extreme of its achievement lies in abstraction. The achievement of the romantic, on the contrary, lies in minor wish-fulfillments and it is incapable of abstraction. In any case and without continuing to contrast the two things, one wants to elicit a sense of the imagination as something vital. In that sense one must deal with it as metaphysics.

If we escape destruction at the hands of the logical positivists and if we cleanse the imagination of the taint of the romantic, we still face Freud. What would he have said of the imagination as the clue to reality and of a culture based on the imagination? Before jumping to the conclusion that at last there is no escape, is it not possible that he might have said that in a civilization based on science there could be a science of illusions? He does in fact say that 'So long as a man's early years are influenced by the religious thought-inhibition . . . as well as by the sexual one, we cannot really say what he is actually like.' If when the primacy of the intelligence has been achieved, one can really say what a man is actually like, what could be more natural than a science of illusions? Moreover, if the imagination is not quite the clue to reality now, might it not become so then? As for the present, what have we, if we do not have science, except the imagination? And who is to say of its deliberate fictions arising out of the contemporary mind that they are not the forerunners of some such science? There is more than the romantic in the statement that the true work of art, whatever it may be, is not the work of

the individual artist. It is time and it is place, as these perfect
themselves.

To regard the imagination as metaphysics is to think of it as
part of life, and to think of it as part of life is to realize the extent
of artifice. We live in the mind. One way of demonstrating what
it means to live in the mind is to imagine a discussion of the
world between two people born blind, able to describe their
images, so far as they have images, without the use of images
derived from other people. It would not be our world that would
be discussed. Still another illustration may help. A man in Paris
does not imagine the same sort of thing that a native of Uganda
imagines. If each could transmit his imagination to the other, so
that the man in Paris, lying awake at night, could suddenly hear
a footfall that meant the presence of some inimical and merciless
monstrosity, and if the man in Uganda found himself in, say, the
Muenster at Basel and experienced what is to be experienced
there, what words would the Parisian find to forestall his fate
and what understanding would the Ugandan have of his incredible delirium? If we live in the mind, we live with the imagination. It is a commonplace to realize the extent of artifice in the
external world and to say that Florence is more imaginative than
Dublin, that blue and white Munich is more imaginative than
white and green Havana, and so on; or to say that, in this town,
no single public object of the imagination exists, while in the
Vatican City, say, no public object exists that is not an object of
the imagination. What is engaging us at the moment has nothing
to do with the external world. We are concerned with the extent
of artifice within us and, almost parenthetically, with the question of its value.

What, then, is it to live in the mind with the imagination, yet
not too near to the fountains of its rhetoric, so that one does not
have a consciousness only of grandeurs, of incessant departures
from the idiom and of inherent altitudes? Only the reason stands
between it and the reality for which the two are engaged in a
struggle. We have no particular interest in this struggle because

we know that it will continue to go on and that there will never be an outcome. We lose sight of it until Pascal, or someone else, reminds us of it. We say that it is merely a routine and the more we think about it the less able we are to see that it has any heroic aspects or that the spirit is at stake or that it may involve the loss of the world. Is there in fact any struggle at all and is the idea of one merely a bit of academic junk? Do not the two carry on together in the mind like two brothers or two sisters or even like young Darby and young Joan? Darby says, 'It is often true that what is most rational appears to be most imaginative, as in the case of Picasso.' Joan replies, 'It is often true, also, that what is most imaginative appears to be most rational, as in the case of Joyce. Life is hard and dear and it is the hardness that makes it dear.' And Darby says, 'Speaking of Joyce and the co-existence of opposites, do you remember the story that Joyce tells of Pascal in *Portrait of the Artist as a Young Man?*[6] Stephen said:

> Pascal, if I remember rightly, would not suffer his mother to kiss him as he feared the contact of her sex –
> Pascal was a pig – said Cranby.
> Aloysius Gonzaga, I think, was of the same mind – Stephen said.
> And he was another pig then – said Cranby.
> The church calls him a saint – Stephen objected.'

How is it that we should be speaking of the prize of the spirit and of the loss, or gain, of the world, in connection with the relations between reason and the imagination? It may be historically true that the reason of a few men has always been the reason of the world. Notwithstanding this, we live today in a time dominated by great masses of men and, while the reason of a few men may underlie what they do, they act as their imaginations impel them to act. The world may, certainly, be lost to the poet but it is not lost to the imagination. I speak of the poet because we think of him as the orator of the imagination. And I say that the world is lost to him, certainly, because, for one thing, the great poems of heaven and hell have been written and the great poem of the earth remains to be written. I suppose it is that poem that will constitute the true prize of the spirit and that until it is written many lesser things will be so regarded, including conquests that are not unimaginable. One wants to consider the imagination on its most momentous scale. Today this scale is not the scale of poetry, nor of any form of literature or art. It is the scale of international politics and in particular of communism. Communism is not the measure of humanity. But I limit myself to an allusion to it as a phenomenon of the imagination. Surely the diffusion of communism exhibits imagination on its most momentous scale. This is because whether or not communism is the measure of humanity, the words themselves echo back to us that it has for the present taken the measure of an important part of humanity. With the collapse of other beliefs, this grubby faith promises a practicable earthly paradise. The only earthly paradise that even the best of the other faiths has been able to promise has been one in man's noblest image and this has always required an imagination that has not yet been included in the fortunes of mankind.

The difference between an imagination that is engaged by the materialism of communism and one that is engaged by the projects of idealism is a difference in nature. It is not that the imagination is versatile but that there are different imaginations. The commonest idea of an imaginative object is something large. But apparently with the Japanese it is the other way round and with them the commonest idea of an imaginative object is something small. With the Hindu it appears to be something vermicular, with the Chinese, something round and with the Dutch, something square. If these evidences do not establish the point, it can hardly be because the point needs establishing. A comparison between the Bible and poetry is relevant. It cannot be said that the Bible, the most widely distributed book in the world, is the poorest. Nor can it be said that it owes its distribution to the poetry it contains. If poetry should address itself to the same needs and aspirations, the same hopes and fears, to which the Bible addresses itself, it might rival it in distribution. Poetry does not address itself to beliefs. Nor could it ever invent an ancient world full of figures that had been known and become endeared to its readers for centuries. Consequently, when critics of poetry call upon it to do some of the things that the Bible does, they overlook the certainty that the Biblical imagination is one thing and the poetic imagination, inevitably, something else. We cannot look at the past or the future except by means of the imagination but again the imagination of backward glances is one thing and the imagination of looks ahead something else. Even the psychologists concede this present particular, for, with them, memory involves a reproductive power, and looks ahead involve a creative power: the power of our expectations. When we speak of the life of the imagination, we do not mean man's life as it is affected by his imagination but the life of the faculty itself. Accordingly, when we think of the permeation of man's life by the imagination, we must not think of it as a life permeated by a single thing but by a class of things. We use our imagination with respect to every man of whom we take notice when by à glance we make up our mind about him. The differences so defined entail differences of value. The imagination that is satisfied by politics, whatever the nature of the politics, has not the same value as the imagination that seeks to satisfy, say, the universal mind, which, in the case of a poet, would be the imagination that tries to penetrate to basic images, basic emotions, and so to compose a fundamental poetry even older than the ancient world. Perhaps one drifts off into rhetoric here, but then there is nothing more congenial than that to the imagination.

Of imaginative life as a social form, let me distinguish at once between everyday living and the activity of cultural organization. A theater is a social form but it is also a cultural organization and it is not my purpose to discuss the imagination as an institution. Having in mind the extent to which the imagination pervades life, it seems curious that it does not pervade, or even create, social form more widely. It is an activity like seeing things or hearing things or any other sensory activity. Perhaps, if one collected instances of imaginative life as social form over a period of time, one might amass a prodigious number from among the customs of our lives. Our social attitudes, social distinctions and the insignia of social distinctions are instances. A ceremonious baptism, a ceremonious wedding, a ceremonious funeral are instances. It takes very little, however, to make a social form arising from the imagination stand out from the normal, and the fact that a form is abnormal is an argument for its suppression. Normal people do not accept something abnormal because it has its origin in an abnormal force like the imagination nor at all until they have somehow normalized it as by familiarity. Costume is an instance of imaginative life as social form. At the same time it is an instance of the acceptance of something incessantly abnormal by reducing it to the normal. It cannot be said that life as we live it from day to day wears an imaginative aspect. On the other hand, it can be said that the aspect of life as we live it from day to day conceals the imagination as social form. No one doubts that the forms of daily living secrete within themselves an infinite variety of things intelligible only to anthropologists nor that lives, like our own, lived after an incalculable number of preceding lives and in the accumulation of what they have left behind are socially complicated even when they appear to be socially innocent. To me, the accumulation of lives at a university has seemed to be a subject that might disclose something extraordinary. What is the residual effect of the years we spend at a university, the years of imaginative life, if ever in our lives there are such years, on the social form of our own future and on the social form of the future of the world of which we are part, when compared with the effects of our later economic and political years?

The discussion of the imagination as metaphysics has led us off a little to one side. This is justified, however, by the considerations, first, that the operation of the imagination in life is more significant than its operation in or in relation to works of art or perhaps I should have said, from the beginning, in arts and letters; second, that the imagination penetrates life; and finally, that its value as metaphysics is not the same as its value in arts and letters. In spite of the prevalence of the imagination in life, it is probably true that the discussion of it in that relation is incomparably less frequent and less intelligent than the discussion of it in relation to arts and letters. The constant discussion of imagination and reality is largely a discussion not for the purposes of life but for the purposes of arts and letters. I suppose that the reason for this is that few people would turn to the imagination, knowingly, in life, while few people would turn to anything else, knowingly, in arts and letters. In life what is important is the truth as it is, while in arts and letters what is important is the truth as we see it. There is a real difference here even though people turn to the imagination without knowing it in life and to reality without knowing it in arts and letters. There are other possible variations of that theme but the theme itself is there. Again in life the function of the imagination is so varied that it is not well-defined as it is in arts and letters. In life one hesitates when one speaks of the value of the imagination. Its value in arts and letters is aesthetic. Most men's lives are thrust upon them. The existence of aesthetic value in lives that are forced on those that live them is an improbable sort of thing. There can be lives, nevertheless, which exist by the deliberate choice of those that live them. To use a single illustration: it may be assumed that the life of Professor Santayana is a life in which the function of the imagination has had a function similar to its function in any deliberate work of art or letters. We have only to think of this present phase of it, in which, in his old age, he dwells in the head of the world, in the company of devoted women, in their convent, and in the company of familiar saints, whose presence does so much to make any convent an appropriate refuge for a generous and human philosopher. To repeat, there can be lives in which the value of the imagination is the same as its value in arts and letters and I exclude from consideration as part of that statement any thought of poverty or wealth, being a *bauer* or being a king, and so on, as irrelevant.

The values of which it is common to think in relation to life are ethical values or moral values. The Victorians thought of these values in relation to arts and letters. It may be that the Russians mean to do about as the Victorians did, that is to say, think of the values of life in relation to arts and letters. A social value is simply an ethical value expressed by a member of the party. Between the wars, we lived, it may be said, in an era when some attempt was made to apply the value of arts and letters to life. These excursions of values beyond their spheres are part of a process which it is unnecessary to delineate. They are like the weather. We suffer from it and enjoy it and never quite know the one feeling from the other. It may, also, be altogether wrong to speak of the excursions of values beyond their spheres, since the question of the existence of spheres and the question of what is appropriate to them are not settled. Thus, something said the other day, that 'An objective theory of value is needed in philosophy which does not depend upon unanalysable intuitions but relates goodness, truth and beauty to human needs in society', has a provocative sound. It is so easy for the poet to say that a learned man must go on being a learned man but that a poet respects no knowledge except his own and, again, that the poet does not yield to the priest. What the poet has in mind, when he says things of this sort, is that poetic value is an intrinsic value. It is not the value of knowledge. It is not the value of faith. It is the value of the imagination. The poet tries to exemplify it, in part, as I have tried to exemplify it here, by identifying it with an imaginative activity that diffuses itself throughout our lives. I say exemplify and not justify, because poetic value is an intuitional value and because intuitional values cannot be justified. We cannot very well speak of spheres of value and the transmission of a value, commonly considered appropriate to one sphere, to another, and allude to the peculiarity of roles, as the poet's role, without reminding ourselves that we are speaking of a thing in continual flux. There is no field in which this is more apparent than painting. Again, there is no field in which it is more constantly and more intelligently the subject of discussion than painting. The permissible reality in painting wavers with an insistence which is itself a value. One might just as well say the permissible imagination. It is as if the painter carried on with himself a continual argument as to whether what delights us in the exercise of the mind is what we produce or whether it is the exercise of a power of the mind.

A generation ago we should have said that the imagination is an aspect of the conflict between man and nature. Today we are more likely to say that it is an aspect of the conflict between men and organized society. It is part of our security. It enables us to live our own lives. We have it because we do not have enough without it. This may not be true as to each one of us, for certainly there are those for whom reality and the reason are enough. It is true of us as a race. A single, strong imagination is like a single, strong reason in this, that the extreme good of each is a spiritual good. It is not possible to say, as between the two, which is paramount. For that matter it is not always possible to say that they are two. When does a building stop being a product of the reason and become a product of the imagination? If we raise a building to an imaginative height, then the building becomes an imaginative building since height in itself is imaginative. It is the moderator of life as metempsychosis was of death. Nietzsche walked in the Alps in the caresses of reality. We ourselves crawl out of our offices and classrooms and become alert at the opera. Or we sit listening to music as in an imagination in which we believe. If the imagination is the faculty by which we import the unreal into what is real, its value is the value of the way of thinking by which we project the idea of God into the idea of man. It creates images that are independent of their originals since nothing is more certain than that the imagination is agreeable to the imagination. When one's aunt in California writes that the geraniums are up to her second-storey window, we soon have them running over the roof. All this diversity, which I have intentionally piled up in confusion in this paragraph, is typical of the imagination. It may suggest that the imagination is the ignorance of the mind. Yet the imagination changes as the mind changes. I know an Italian who was a shepherd in Italy as a boy. He described his day's work. He said that at evening he was so tired he would lie down under a tree like a dog. This image was, of course, an image of his own dog. It was easy for him to say how tired he was by using the image of his tired dog. But given another mind, given the mind of a man of strong powers, accustomed to thought, accustomed to the essays of the imagination, and the whole imaginative substance changes. It is as if one could say that the imagination lives as the mind lives. The primitivism disappears. The Platonic resolution of diversity appears. The world is no longer an extraneous object, full of other extraneous objects, but an image. In the last analysis, it is with this image of the world that we are vitally concerned. We should not say, however, that the chief object of the imagination is to produce such an image. Among so many objects, it would be the merest improvisation to say of one, even though it is one with which we are vitally concerned, that it is the chief. The next step would be to assert that a particular image was the chief image. Again, it would be the merest improvisation to say of any image of the world, even though it was an image with which a vast accumulation of imaginations had been content, that it was the chief image. The imagination itself would not remain content with it nor allow us to do so. It is the irrepressible revolutionist.

In spite of the confusion of values and the diversity of aspects, one arrives eventually face to face with arts and letters. I could take advantage of the pictures from the Kaiser Friedrich Museum in Berlin, which are being exhibited throughout the country and which many of you, no doubt, have seen. The pictures by Poussin[7] are not the most marvelous pictures in this collection. Yet, considered as objects of the imagination, how completely they validate Gide's:[8] 'We must approach Poussin little by little' and how firmly they sustain the statement made a few moments ago that the imagination is the only genius. There is also among these pictures a Giorgione,[9] the portrait of a young man, head and shoulders, in a blue-purple blouse, or if not blue-purple, then a blue of extraordinary enhancings. Vasari[10] said of Giorgione that he painted nothing that he had not seen in nature. This portrait is an instance of a real object that is at the same time an imaginative object. It has about it an imaginative bigness of diction. We know that in poetry bigness and gaiety are precious characteristics of the diction. This portrait transfers that principle to painting. The subject is severe but its embellishment, though no less severe, is big and gay and one feels in the presence of this work that one is also in the presence of an abundant and joyous spirit, instantly perceptible in what may be called the diction of the portrait. I could also take advantage, so far as letters are concerned, of a few first books of poems or a few first novels. One turns to first works of the imagination with the same expectation with which one turns to last works of the reason. But I am afraid that although one is, at last, face to face with arts and letters and, therefore, in the presence of particulars beyond particularization, it is prudent to limit discussion to a single point.

My final point, then, is that the imagination is the power that enables us to perceive the normal in the abnormal, the opposite of chaos in chaos. It does this every day in arts and letters. This may seem to be a merely capricious statement; for ordinarily we regard the imagination as abnormal per se. That point of view was approached in the reference to the academic struggle between reason and the imagination and again in the reference to the relation between imagination and social form. The disposition toward a point of view derogatory to the imagination is an aversion to the abnormal. We see it in the common attitude toward modern arts and letters. The exploits of Rimbaud[11] in poetry, if Rimbaud can any longer be called modern, and of Kafka[12] in prose are deliberate exploits of the abnormal. It is natural for us to identify the imagination with those that extend its abnormality. It is like identifying liberty with those that abuse it. A literature overfull of abnormality and, certainly, present-day European literature, as one knows it, seems to be a literature full of abnormality, gives the reason an appearance of normality to which it is not, solely, entitled. The truth seems to be that we live in concepts of the imagination before the reason has established them. If this is true, then reason is simply the methodizer of the imagination. It may be that the imagination is a miracle of logic and that its exquisite divinations are calculations beyond analysis, as the conclusions of the reason are calculations wholly within analysis. If so, one understands perfectly the remark that 'in the service of love and imagination nothing can be too lavish, too sublime or too festive'. In the statement that we live in concepts of the imagination before the reason has established them, the word 'concepts' means concepts of normality. Further, the statement that the imagination is the power that enables us to perceive the normal in the abnormal is a form of repetition of this statement. One statement does not demonstrate the other. The two statements together imply that the instantaneous disclosures of living are disclosures of the normal. This will seem absurd to those that insist on the solitude and misery and terror of the world. They will ask of what value is the imagination to them; and if their experience is to be considered, how is it possible to deny that they live in an imagination of evil? Is evil normal or abnormal? And how do the exquisite divinations of the poets and for that matter even the 'aureoles of the saints' help them? But when we speak of perceiving the normal we have in mind the instinctive integrations which are the reason for living. Of what value is anything to the solitary and those that live in misery and terror, except the imagination?

Jean Paulhan,[13] a Frenchman and a writer, is a man of great sense. He is a native of the region of Tarbes. Tarbes is a town in southwestern France in the High Pyrenees. Marshal Foch[14] was born there. An equestrian statue of the Marshal stands there, high in the air, on a pedestal. In his *Les Fleurs de Tarbes*, Jean Paulhan says:

> One sees at the entrance of the public garden of Tarbes, this sign:

IT IS FORBIDDEN
TO ENTER INTO THE GARDEN
CARRYING FLOWERS.

He goes on to say:

> One finds it, also, in our time at the portal of literature. Nevertheless, it would be agreeable to see the girls of Tarbes (and the young writers) carrying a rose, a red poppy, an armful of red poppies.

I repeat that Jean Paulhan is a man of great sense. But to be able to see the portal of literature, that is to say: the portal of the imagination, as a scene of normal love and normal beauty is, of itself, a feat of great imagination. It is the vista a man sees, seated in the public garden of his native town, near by some effigy of a figure celebrated in the normal world, as he considers that the chief problems of any artist, as of any man, are the problems of the normal and that he needs, in order to solve them, everything that the imagination has to give.

Notes

1 Blaise Pascal's (1623–62) *Pensées*, a collection of thoughts and meditations, were edited and published by friends of the author in 1670.

2 Ernst Cassirer (1874–1945), German neo-Kantian philosopher. After fleeing Nazi Germany, he taught in England, Sweden and the USA. *An Essay on Man* appeared in 1944.

3 Walter Horatio Pater (1839–94), Oxford don and author of *Studies in the History of the Renaissance* (1873).

4 Alfred Jules Ayer (b. 1910), Professor of Logic at Oxford, steered English philosophy away from metaphysics towards language analysis; *Language, Truth and Logic* was published in 1936.

5 Cyril Edwin Mitchinson Joad (1891–1953), philosopher, author, teacher, and champion of unpopular causes. Although he was a rationalist in the mould of H. G. Wells and G. B. Shaw, towards the end of his life his writings took on a religious dimension; *Recovery of Belief* was published in 1952.

6 James Joyce (1882–1941) published *A Portrait of the Artist as a Young Man* in 1916.

7 Nicolas Poussin (1594–1665), the French painter; his *Saint Matthew and the Angel* is in Berlin.

8 André Gide (1869–1951), the French novelist.

9 Giorgione (1477/8–1510), the painter of the Venetian Renaissance, is said to have introduced the 'modern' style of the sixteenth century with new effects of colour and light.

10 Giorgio Vasari (1511–1574), Italian painter, architect and writer, most important for his history of the art of the Italian Renaissance, *The Lives of the Most Eminent Italian Architects, Painters and Sculptors* (1550).

11 Arthur Rimbaud (1854–91), the French poet, retired from literature at the age of nineteen.

12 Franz Kafka (1883–1924), the Austrian novel, fable and parable writer.

13 Jean Paulhan (1884–1968), French writer and director of the important journal *La Nouvelle Revue Française*. The study

of literature and language, *Les Fleurs de Tarbes*, appeared in 1941.

14 Ferdinand Foch (1851–1929), Marshal of France, Great Britain and Poland, and author of *The Principles of War*.

Andrei Bely

Andrei Bely is the pseudonym of Boris Nikolaevich Bugaev (1880–1934), the son of a strong-minded professor of mathematics at Moscow University and a tense, emotional mother. His childhood was impressed by the quarrelling of his incompatible parents. He grew up in Moscow and studied natural science, then philosophy, reading Vladimir Solovyov, Nietzsche, Kant and theosophical literature. After 1913 he was an adept of Rudolf Steiner and anthroposophy. From the beginning of the century, with the Petersburg writers Aleksandr Blok and Vyacheslav Ivanov and the Muscovite Valery Bryusov, he distinguished himself as one of the major voices of Russian symbolism. Though he wrote much poetry, his major achievement lies in the novel and in critical and philosophical literature.

WRITINGS

These include countless articles and about fifty books; four works of prose fiction, *The Four Symphonies* (1901–8); the novels *The Silver Dove* (1909), *Petersburg* (1913–14) and *Kotik Letaev* (1916); a narrative poem, *First Meeting*; the critical and speculative volumes *Symbolism* (1910) and *Arabesques* (1911); an essay on sound symbolism, *Glossaloliya* (1922); and a critical study, *Gogol's Craftsmanship* (1934); also four important books of memoirs.

'The Magic of Words' was written in 1909 as a lecture to the

Society of Free Aesthetics and was printed subsequently in *Symbolism*.

THE MAGIC OF WORDS

I

Language is the most powerful instrument of creation. In naming an object with a word I assert its existence. All knowledge results from the naming. Knowledge is not possible without the word. The process of knowing something is the forging of relationships between words which are subsequently transferred to objects which correspond to the words. Grammatical forms, which make sentence construction possible, are possible only when words exist; the logical articulation of speech occurs only later. In asserting that creation precedes knowledge I assert the primacy of creation, not only in its epistemological priority but also in its genetic sequence.

Figurative speech is made up of words which express logically my inexpressible impression of the things that surround me. Living speech is always the music of the inexpressible. 'A thought that is spoken is a lie', says Tyutchev,[1] and he is right if, by a thought, he understands something that is expressed in a series of terminological concepts. But the living, spoken word is not a lie. It is the expression of the secret essence of my nature, and, inasmuch as my nature is nature in general, the word is an expression of the innermost secrets of nature. Every word is a sound. I can understand the spatial and causal relationships outside me by means of the word. If words did not exist, the world would not exist either. Isolated from its surroundings, my 'I' does not exist at all; nor does the world exist, isolated from me; 'I' and 'world' come into being only in the process of their joining through sound. Consciousness and nature which lie outside the individual become contiguous and are joined only in the process of naming. Thus consciousness, nature and world come into being for the knower only when he is able to create names; there is no nature, world or knower outside language. Primal creation is inherent in the word; the word links the wordless, invisible world, which swarms in the subconscious depths of my personal consciousness, with the wordless, meaningless world which swarms outside my person. The word creates a new, third world, a world of sound symbols through which the secrets of the worlds, confined both outside and inside me, are illuminated. Then the outside world pours into my soul just as the inside world spills over into the dawn, into the rustle of trees; I re-create for myself all that surrounds me, on the outside and the inside, through words and only through words, for I am a *word* and only a *word*.

But the word is a symbol; it is the combination, in a way comprehensible to me, of two essences that are in themselves incomprehensible: space, accessible to my vision, and that hollow-sounding feeling within me to which I give the conventional (formal) name of time. Two analogies are created simultaneously in the word: time is depicted by an external phenomenon – by sound; space is depicted by the same phenomenon, again by sound. But the *sound of space* is already its inner re-creation; *sound* joins time and space, but in a way that reduces spatial relationships to temporal ones; by creating such relationships anew, I am freed, in a certain sense, from the power of space; sound is the objectification of time and space. Yet every *word* is first of all a *sound*; the primeval victory of consciousness lies in the creation of sound symbols. In sound a new world is created within whose bounds I feel myself to be the creator of reality; then I begin to name objects, that is, re-create them a second time for myself. In attempting to give a name to all that comes to my attention I am, essentially, defending myself against the world which is hostile and unknown to me, putting pressure on me from all sides; I subdue these hostile elements with the sound of a word. The process of assigning words to spatial and temporal phenomena is the process of an incantation; each word is the casting of a spell – in *casting a spell* on a phenomenon I am, in fact, subduing it; and thus the connection between words, their grammatical and representational forms, lies in the act of casting a spell; naming the sound of thunder, which frightens me, 'thunder', I create a sound which imitates thunder ('thunnd');* in creating such a sound I begin to re-create thunder, so to speak; this process of re-creation *is* knowledge. At bottom, I am casting a spell on thunder. The joining of words, a sequence of sounds in time, inevitably suggests causality. Causality is the joining of space with time. *Sound* is the symbol of both space and time; defined externally, sound joins space and time in this sense: uttering a sound requires a moment of time; moreover: a sound always resounds in the *environment*, for sound is the *resounding environment*. Space and time are contiguous in *sound* and thus sound is the root of all causality; the connection between sound signs always imitates those between phenomena in space and time.

Thus the word always engenders causality; it creates causal relationships which subsequently become the object of knowledge.

Causal explanation in the very first stages of mankind's development is only a creation of words; a sorcerer is one who knows more words than others and who speaks well and thus

---

* By no means all word formation proceeds from onomatopoeic elements; the symbolism of language is incomparably subtler and deeper. About this, see Potebnya's *Notes on Russian Grammar*.[2] For defining word creation we have rich material in comparative linguistics; and, further, in the history of the development of living languages. All this material, however, still tells us nothing essential about primordial forms of speech; every conclusion drawn from the laws of the development of known languages and applied to the history of the development of primordial speech is a conclusion by analogy and analogy alone. We can consider the process of living speech; it is worth looking more closely at the origin of new words in order to learn from within about the process of the formation of living speech. The psychology of poetic (mythic) creation and the historical material mark two extreme points between which all conclusions about the creation of language will vary.

casts a spell. It is not for nothing that magic acknowledges the power of words. Living speech itself is uninterrupted magic. I can fathom the essence of phenomena more deeply with a successfully created word than with analytical thought; I distinguish phenomena with such thought, whereas, with the *word*, I gain control over phenomena; the creation of living speech is always man's struggle with the hostile elements that surround him; the word sets the darkness about me ablaze with the light of victory.

It follows that living language is a condition for the existence of mankind itself; this condition is the quintessence of mankind itself; and this is why poetry, knowledge, music and speech were at first a unity; and this is why living language was magic, and why people who spoke such a language were impressed with the stamp of communion with deity itself. It is significant that ancient legends hint, in various ways, at the existence of a magic language whose words enchant and subdue nature; it is significant that each of the sacred hieroglyphs in Egypt had a triple meaning; the first meaning was identified with a word's sound which gave a name to the hieroglyphic image (time); the second meaning was identified with the spatial outline of the sound (the image), that is, with the hieroglyph; the third meaning was contained in a sacred number which symbolized the word. Fabre d'Olivet[3] has successfully attempted to decipher the symbolic meaning of the name of the Jewish deity. He writes of the myth of the holy dialect 'Zenzar' in which mankind was made aware of the greatest of revelations. The natural conclusions and the myths about language, independent of their degree of objectivity, both express man's involuntary striving to symbolize the magic power of the word.

Potebnya and Afanasev[4] cite a number of folk sayings where the sound of a word determines thought processes more than one would expect: 11 May is the memorial day to the renewal of the city of Tsargrad [*Tsar* = King; *grad* = city, hail]; in the country the idea took root that one should not work in the field on this day lest '*Tsar grad* [King hail] beat down the corn'; 16 June is St Tikhon's [*tikhi*= slow, still, quiet] day – whence the saying 'the sun moves more *slowly* [*tishe*], song birds *quieten down* [*zatikhayut*]'; 2 February is Candlemas (*Sretenie*) – 'winter and summer have met [*vstretilis*]'. . . .

Mankind's calling is the active creation of life. The life of mankind presupposes communication between individuals, but communication is made through words and only through words. All communication is an active creative process where souls exchange with each other their most treasured images which portray and construct life's secrets. The purpose of communication is to set alight, through the contact of two inner worlds, a third world which is identical for those who communicate and which unexpectedly deepens the individual images of the soul. For this it is necessary that the word of communication not be an abstract concept. An abstract concept definitively crystallizes acts of knowledge which have already taken place. But mankind's purpose is to create the objects of knowledge themselves; the purpose of communication is to kindle the signs of communication, i.e. the words, with the fire of ever new creative processes. The purpose of living communication is the striving towards the future; thus, abstract words, when they become the signs of communication, refer communication between people to what has already been; conversely the living language of images which we hear sets our imagination alight with the fire of new creations, that is, new word formations; a word formation is always the beginning of new knowledge.

Poetic language is language in the true sense of the word; its main significance lies in the fact that it attempts to prove nothing with words; poetic language gathers words whose sum total yields an image; the logical significance of this image is undefined; the image is also undefined visually so that we ourselves must fill the living language with knowledge and creation; the perception of a living language of images spurs us on to creative activity; in every living man this language sets off a sequence of activity; and a poetic image is created completely – by each individual. Figurative speech engenders images; each man becomes a bit of an artist on hearing the living word. The living word (metaphor, simile, epithet) is a seed germinating in the soul; it promises thousands of flowers; in one soul it grows up as a white rose, in another as a blue cornflower. The meaning of living speech lies not at all in its logical significance – logic itself is a product of speech; it is not without reason that the condition for logical assertions is the creative imperative to regard them as such for particular purposes; but these purposes do not by any means cover the real purpose of language as the organ of communication. The main task of speech is to create new images and permeate people's souls with their shining splendour so as to cover the world with this splendour. The evolution of language is by no means a systematic elimination of the figurative content of words; a word without figurative content is an abstract concept; an abstract concept terminates the process of man's subjugation of nature; in this sense, mankind, at certain stages of development, raises temples of knowledge out of living language. Then there follows a new need for creation. The 'word-seed' which had sunk into the depths of the unconsciousness swells and bursts out of its dry shell (a concept), sending up a new shoot; this animation of the word points to a new organic period of culture; yesterday's elders of culture, under the pressure of new words, abandon their temples, return to the woods and fields in order to cast a spell on and subdue nature again; the word sheds its conceptual shell and gleams with an unspoilt, barbaric diversity of colours.

Such periods are accompanied by the intrusion of poetry into the realm of terminological language, and by an intrusion of the spirit of music into poetry; the musical power of sound is reborn in the word; once again we are captivated not by the meaning but by the sound of words; in this enthusiasm we unconsciously sense that the deepest vital meaning of the word, concealed in the very expression of sound and image – is to be a creative word. The creative word constructs the world.*

The creative word is a word incarnate (the word is flesh) and, in this sense, it is real; the living flesh of man serves as its symbol; the word-term is a skeleton; no one would begin to deny the importance of an osteologist; his knowledge is necessary and serves a practical need in life; a knowledge of anatomy is, above all, one of the prerequisites for treating illness (one must be able to straighten out humps, set broken bones, etc.); but no one would claim that the skeleton is the central axis of a culture. In attributing primary rather than a secondary and auxiliary importance to the terminological significance of the word, we kill language, i.e. the living word; there is an uninterrupted exercise of the creative powers of language in the living word; in essence we exercise power in creating and combining sound images. Though we may be told that such exercise is a game, is not a game really an exercise in creation? A specific variety of forms always emerges from such a game; the game itself is a vital instinct; in sporting games, muscles are exercised and strengthened – a combatant needs muscles when encountering his enemy; in living speech the creative power of the mind is exercised and strengthened for it is needed when mankind is threatened. Thus, though it seems ridiculous to the undeveloped ear, the exercise of the mind in combining the sounds of words has an enormous significance; in the creation of words, in the naming of unknown phenomena, we subdue and enchant these phenomena with sounds; all life is sustained by the vital power of speech; outside speech we have no direct signs for communication; all other signs (whether lively gestures or abstract emblems) are only secondary, auxiliary means of speech. All of them amount to nothing in the face of a living language; living language is an eternally flowing, creative activity, which raises before us a series of images and myths; our

* In Christian mysticism this meaning of the word is underlined by the apostle John: 'In the beginning was the Word, and the Word was with God, and the Word was God.'. . .

consciousness derives power and confidence from these images; they are weapons with which we penetrate darkness. As darkness is defeated, images disintegrate and the poetry of words is gradually worn away; already we identify words with abstract concepts, though above all not in order to convince ourselves of the purposelessness of the images of language; we break down living language into concepts in order to tear them away from life, pack them into thousands of tomes and leave them to rest in the dust of archives and libraries. Then vital life, deprived of vital words, becomes madness and chaos for us; space and time begin to threaten us again; new clouds of the unknown, having drifted up to the horizon of what has been identified, menace us with fire and lightning, threaten to sweep humankind from the face of the earth. Then there follows a period of so-called degeneration; man comes to see that terms have not saved him. Blinded by imminent destruction, man in terror begins to cast a spell with the word over the unknown dangers; to his astonishment he recognizes only in words the means for real incantation; then beneath the crust of the worn-out words a bright stream of new word meanings gushes forth. New words are created. Degeneration is transformed into a healthy barbarism. The cause of the degeneration is the death of the living word; the struggle with degeneration is the creation of new words. In all declines of culture, regeneration has been preceded and accompanied by a special cult of words; the cult of words is the active cause of new creation. A limited awareness invariably confuses cause with effect; the cause (the death of the living word), having been called the effect (the counteraction of the death through the cult of the word), is confused with the effect; the creative cult of the word is invariably linked with degeneration; on the contrary: degeneration is the result of the extinction of words. The cult of the word is the beginning of regeneration.

The word-term is a beautiful and dead crystal formed as a result of the completion of the decaying process of the living word. The living word (word-flesh) is a flourishing organism.

All that is felt in me by my senses decays when I die; my body becomes a rotting corpse which stinks; but when the process of decay ends I appear before the gaze of those who have loved me in a row of beautiful crystals. The ideal term is an eternal crystal obtained only by way of its final decay. The word-image is like a living human being; it creates, affects and changes its content. An ordinary, prosaic word, one having lost its sound and descriptive imagery and not having as yet become an ideal term, is a stinking, rotting corpse.

There are few ideal terms because there have been so few living words; all our life is filled with rotting words which give off an unbearable stink; the use of these words infects us with the poison of a corpse, because the word is the direct expression of life.

And thus the only thing to which our vitality commits us is the creation of words. We must harness our power in the combining of words; in so doing we forge a weapon with which to combat the living corpses which impinge upon our activities; we must become barbarians, executioners of the popular word, if we cannot first breathe life into it. The word-term is another matter – it does not claim to be alive; it is what it is – you can't bring it back to life, but it is harmless; the poison itself of the corpse has decayed into an ideal term so that it cannot infect anyone.

The stinking word, half image, half term, neither one thing nor the other, rotting carrion pretending to be alive, is another matter: it is a werewolf, creeps into our everyday life in order to undermine the power of creation with the false claim that creation is a barren combination of words, in order to undermine the power of our knowledge with the false claim that knowledge is a barren catalogue of terms. Perhaps those who assert that the figurativeness of language is a purposeless play with words are right, because we do not see a tangible meaning in the selection of words according to sound and image. The 'purposiveness' of such a selection is purposiveness without a purpose; how strange it is that a brilliant thinker like Kant,[5] who values works

of art so highly, defines art with this word, and one of the best
music critics (Hanslick)[6] defines music similarly: either Hanslick and Kant are mad or their words are addressed to some
absolute reality of art. Purposiveness in art has no purpose
within the confines of art, for the goal of art is rooted in the
creation of the very objects of knowledge; one must either
transform life into art or make art something that lives; then the
meaning of art is revealed and consecrated. In regard to poetry,
for example, this is true in the sense that the purpose of poetry is
the creation of language; and language is the very creation of
living relationships. If word-play has no purpose, then we adopt
a purely aesthetic point of view; but when we realize that
aesthetics is only a facet, which refracts the creation of life in its
own way, and, in itself, beyond this creation, has no part to play,
then the purposeless play with words turns out to be full of
meaning: a combination of words, irrespective of their logical
meaning, is the means by which man defends himself from the
pressure of the unknown. Armed with the defence of words,
man re-creates everything he sees, invades the limits of the
unknown like a warrior and, if he triumphs, his words thunder,
flare up with the sparks of constellations, shroud his listeners
with the darkness of interplanetary space, send them off to an
unknown planet where rainbows gleam, rivers murmur and
huge cities tower up, in which his listeners, as though dreaming,
find themselves exhausted in a four-cornered enclosure called a
room, where they dream that someone is speaking to them; they
think the *word* of the speaker comes from the speaker; and that it
is authentic. If this is how it seems to them, then the magic of
words has been realized and the illusion of knowledge begins to
have an effect; it then begins to seem that there is some hidden
meaning behind the words, that knowledge is separable from
the word; but meanwhile the whole dream of knowledge has
been created by the word; the knower always speaks aloud or
mentally; all knowledge is an illusion which follows the word:
word combinations and sound analogies (for example, the sub-

stitution of space for time and time for space) arise already in figurative forms of speech; if speech did not take shape in the form of metaphor, metonymy or synechdoche, Kant's doctrine of the category of pure concepts of reason would not exist, because his is neither doctrine nor knowledge but merely a verbal exposition and nothing more. He who speaks is he who creates; if he speaks with confidence, it begins to seem to him that he knows, and those whom his words affect feel they are also involved; in the strict sense, there are no pupils and no teachers, no knowers and no knowables; the knower is always the undefined roar of the wordless soul; the knowable is the counter-roar of the elements of life; only the fireworks of words which explode at the border of two non-contiguous voids create the illusion of knowledge; yet this knowledge is not knowledge but the creation of a new world in sound. Sound itself is indivisible, omnipotent, unalterable; but mixed choruses of sounds and the confused echoes of sound recalled by the memory begin to weave a veil of eternal illusion; we call this illusion knowledge, until our knowledge, having completely banished sound, becomes a dumb word or a dumb mathematical sign for us.

Knowledge becomes a catalogue of dumb and empty words – dumb, because they have nothing to say, empty, because all content has been removed from them; this is what the fundamental concepts of epistemology are, or, at least, what they try to be; these concepts want to be free of all psychical life – but there is no sound outside psychical life, no word, no life, no creation. Knowledge proves to be ignorance.

In the forthright reduction of knowledge, just as in the forthright combination of sounds for sounds' sake, there is more frankness and integrity than in the cowardly way in which one holds on to words stinking with decay, to words that are neither forthrightly figurative nor forthrightly flourishing. Every science, if it is not forthrightly mathematical and not forthrightly *terminological*, leads us to deception, degeneration and lies; all living language, if it is not openly intoxicated with the verbal fireworks of sounds and images, is not a living language but a language impregnated with the poison of corpses.

Let us speak candidly: there is no knowledge in the sense of an explanation of phenomena with the word; thus scientific discoveries, based on experiment, have at their root the creation of sound analogies, which are externalized and taken for an effect. What is an experiment? It always has to do with an *action* which combines conditions of nature in a distinctive way. We take a magnet (action), place it in a wire bobbin (action); we obtain the phenomena of electromagnetism (action); as yet there are no words, but we will be told: the phenomena of electromagnetism are explicable verbally; we answer bluntly that they are not explained; the realm of explanation is one of a construction of word analogies; a verbal explanation of an experiment turns into an explanation that relies on formulas; but a formula is already a gesture, a dumb sign; an explanation of the formula with words is one which relies on analogies; analogy is not yet knowledge.

And, conversely, if one proves that the experiment originates from words, this is not yet proof of the origin of exact science from abstract concepts. Every living word is the magic of an incantation; no one can prove that it is not possible to assume that the first experiment, called forth by a word, is itself a calling forth, an incantation by means of the word of a phenomenon which has never existed; the word engenders action; the action is the continuation of a mythic construction.

The worlds of abstract concepts, like the worlds of essences, regardless of what we call these essences (matter, spirit, nature), are not real; they do not exist without the word; the word is the only real vessel on which we travel from one unknown to another, through unknown spaces called earth, sky, ether, emptiness, etc., through unknown times, called gods, demons, souls. We don't know what matter, earth, sky, air are; we don't know what god, demon, soul are; we call something 'I', 'you', 'he'; but in naming the unknowns with words we create a world for ourselves; the word is a spell cast over things; the word is the call and the calling forth of a god. When I say 'I', I create a sound symbol; I assert that this symbol exists; only in this moment do I become conscious of myself.

All knowledge is the fireworks of words with which I fill the emptiness surrounding me; if my words sparkle with colours, they create the illusion of light; and this illusion of light *is* knowledge. No one convinces anyone. No one proves anything to anyone; every argument is a battle of words, is magic; I speak only in order to cast a spell; a battle with words which has the appearance of a dispute is the filling up of emptiness with one thing or the other: at this point it is normal to silence an opponent with rotten words; but this is not persuasion – the opponent, upon returning home after the argument, is sickened by the rotten words. In early times emptiness was filled with light by the fires of images; this was the process of mythic creation. The word gave rise to the descriptive symbol – the metaphor; the metaphor seemed to be something that really existed; the word gave rise to myth, and myth gave rise to religion, religion to philosophy, and philosophy to the term.

It is better to shoot off word-rockets purposelessly into emptiness than to allow dust to gather in the same place. The former is the effect of living language, the latter, that of dead language. We often prefer the latter. We are half alive, half dead.

II

The entire process of creative symbolization is already contained in the means of representation present in language itself. In language, as activity, the means of representation are the organic beginning; on the one hand they directly influence the development of grammatical forms: the transition from *epitheton ornans* to the adjective is imperceptible; every adjective is an epithet in a certain sense; every epithet is essentially similar to one or another more complex form (metaphor, metonymy, synecdoche). Potebnya demonstrates, not without foundation, that every epithet (*ornans*) is at the same time a synecdoche; on the other hand, he does cite cases when the synecdoche is coextensive with metonymy; in metonymy we already have the tendency to create knowledge itself; the content of many causal interactions we bring about arises initially from several metonymic combinations of images (where space is transferred to time and time to space; where the meaning of the metonymic image arises from the fact that the cause is already contained in its effect or the effect in its cause). On the other hand, Aristotle reckons synecdoche and metonymy to be particular cases of the metaphor.

Potebnya points to a number of typical cases of inference in the realm of metaphor, metonymy and synecdoche: we can cite a couple of such cases (taken from *Notes on the Theory of Literature*).

In the realm of metaphor: (1) 'a' is similar to 'b'; hence 'a' is the cause of 'b' (a *sound* is the phenomenon of hearing; thus a *sound* in the ear of an absent person comes as a result of speaking about it; a whistle is wind, hence sorcerers call the wind forth with a whistle); (2) the image becomes the cause of the phenomenon: a *pearl* is similar to a drop of dew [cf. the phrase 'pearly dew']; consequently *dew* gives rise to the pearl, etc. All mythical thought has taken shape under the influence of the creation of language; the image in myth becomes the cause of existing outward appearance; hence the creation of language passes into philosophy; philosophy, in this sense, is the growth and further particularization of myth.

Figures of speech are not separable one from another – they are interconnected; in certain figures of speech a number of forms coincide: metaphor, metonymy and synecdoche coincide with the epithet. On the other hand, the broadest definition of the metaphor is that which includes synecdoche and metonymy. In the *epithet*, the synecdoche combines in itself metaphor and metonymy. Finally there exists a series of transitions between simile and metaphor, for example, the expression 'the cloud, like a mountain' is a typical simile; the expression 'the heavenly mountain' (in reference to a cloud) is a typical metaphor; in the expression 'a cloud-mountain floats about the sky' ['*tucha goroyu plyvet po nebu*'],[7] there is a transition from simile to metaphor; in the words 'a cloud-mountain' ['*tucha goroyu*'], a simile encounters a metaphor; or in the expressions 'stormy eyes', 'eyes like a storm', 'eye-storms' ['*ochi grozoyu*'], 'the storm of eyes' (instead of a glance), we have all stages of transition from epithet to metaphor, made by means of a simile. Hence the particularization of the means of representation is interesting from the point of view of psychological transition in time from a given object to its figurative assimilation.

Something more general happens in these figures of speech, namely, the striving to enlarge the verbal representation of a given image, to make its boundaries unstable, to create a new cycle of verbal creation, i.e. to give a jolt to ordinary verbal representation, to impart movement to its inner form. The alteration of a word's inner form leads to the creation of new content in the image; then a spaciousness is given to our creative perception of reality; this expansion occurs when, apparently, we are concerned formally with the analysis of the representation of an object. When we say 'the moon is white', we add one of several signs to the moon; but the moon is also golden, red, full and pointed, etc. We may break the moon down into a series of qualities, but we must remember that such reduction of the representation of the moon, as a set of signs, is the beginning of a process. We disassemble, as it were, the representation of the moon in order to join each element in the set with the discarded sets of other representations in one, two or more signs; analysis here is predefined as a requirement for synthesis; singling out the whiteness of the moon from its many signs we dwell on this one, only because it fixes the direction of the creative process: having chosen the *whiteness of the moon* as a point of departure, we can group other signs around this one; noticing that the moon is most frequently white in the evening when it is crescent shaped, we define it by adding a new epithet: the *white, pointed moon*. The representation of the moon narrows, becomes concrete, and involuntarily we compare the moon to many pointed, white objects (a white horn, a white tusk, etc.). Here we are joining two opposed objects in one or two signs: (1) a *white, pointed* (pertaining to animals) *horn*, (2) *white, pointed* (celestial, not pertaining to animals) moon; we compare the moon to a horn; *the moon, like a white, pointed horn*. In this way the transition from epithet to *simile* is necessary. The simile is the next stage in the creation of images.

The comparison of objects based on one or more signs leads to a new stage: in the comparison we introduce to the field of our vision a complex set of signs; two objects, two conflicting representations, stand before us; and, according to Potebnya, we see three ways out of this conflict: 'A' entirely included in 'X' (synecdoche); 'A' partially included in 'X' (metonymy); 'A' and 'X' not directly related, joined by 'B' (metaphor); in all three cases either a transference of one perception of the object to another – a quantitative one (synecdoche), a qualitative one (metonymy) – or a substitution of the objects themselves (metaphor) takes place. As a result of the conflict we obtain the dual form of the *metaphor*; we obtain an epithetic form when the representation of the object compared dominates the object to which the first object (moon) is compared (*white-horned* moon); the epithet *white-horned* is obtained from a comparison of the *whiteness* of the moon with the *whiteness* of a horn; this gives rise to the following schema:

A *Moon* — (a_1) white, (a_2) pointed $\Big\}$ *White-horned moon*
B *Horn* — (b_1) white, (b_2) pointed $\Big/$ (a_1, b_2, B–A)

Two homogeneous signs of the heterogeneous sets (moon, horn) are joined in the first half of the epithet (white-); in the second half of the epithet (-pointed) the set of signs (horn) is transformed into one of the signs of the other object (moon); the epithet *white-horned* is, in itself, a synecdoche because the species (white horn) is identified with the genus (a horn can be yellow or white or black); adding to the epithet 'white-horned' the name of the object 'moon', we obtain a metaphor because the synecdochic epithet 'white-horned' is joined with the representation of the moon so that the meaning 'white-horned' is ascribed to a new object (instead of 'white-horned goat', 'white-horned moon').

Or, we obtain another form of metaphor: 'the moon is a white horn' or 'the white horn in the sky'. Here the object with which some of the qualities of the moon were compared has supplanted this object itself; the formulation of the image can follow two directions: either the representation of the *white horn* in the sky supplants both the representation of the horn (belonging to an earthly creature) and the normal representation of the moon (not as a part of some whole but as a whole); and we obtain some symbol equally unrelated to both moon and horn; or the representation of the white horn in the sky takes another form: 'the moon-white horn in the sky'. Returning to the schema above we have:

A *Moon* — (a_1) white, (a_2) pointed   *Moon-white horn*
B *Horn* — (b_1) white, (b_2) pointed   (A, a_1, b_1 – B)

In the first half of the epithet (moon-) a set of signs (the moon) is joined as one of the signs of the object (the horn), in the second half of the epithet (-white), two homogeneous signs of the two heterogeneous objects are joined; the epithet 'moon-white' is a synecdoche; moon-white horn is at once metaphor and metonymy (metonymy because it is a lunar horn); the substitution, assuming the process of the metaphorical assimilation completed and ascribed to the horn, points to (1) the definition of the genus by the *species* (a horn defined by the white horn), (2) a qualitative distinction of objects (a lunar *horn* qualitatively distinct from any other horn).

One and the same process of depiction which passes through

distinct phases will appear to us as an epithet, then a simile, then a synecdoche, then a metonymy, then a metaphor, in the narrow sense of these words.

We express these psychological phases of successive transition from certain forms to others in a series of schemas:

Moon = A, horn = B, white = a_1 b_1; pointed = a_2 b_2. Thus:
A – a_1, a_2
B – b_1, b_2

The case of the complex epithet:
a_1, a_2 – A = white-pointed moon
b_1, b_2 – B = white-pointed horn

The case of the simile:
A – a_1 B = the moon, like a white horn
B – b_1 A = the horn, like a white moon
But 'a_1 = b_1' (white = white)

Hence the case of the metaphor:
A = B ∴ the moon is a horn
B = A ∴ the horn is a moon

Between the simile and the metaphor secondary processes of word formations can occur (synecdoche, metonymy).

The case of the synecdoche:
a_1 B – A = white-horned moon
b_1 A – B = white-moon horn

The latter case is at the same time a *metonymy*:

The case of the metonymy:
b_1 A – B = white-moon horn

Finally, in the epithetic form 'AB' = moon-horned, we obtain all three forms at once: metaphor, metonymy, synecdoche, depending on where the epithet is placed. In itself the epithet *moon-horned* is a metaphorical epithet; like every *epitheton ornans*, it is, moreover, according to Potebnya, also a synecdoche; when we say 'the moon-horned goat' we not only refer a species (the goat) to the genus (animals with horns) but also attribute to the individuals of this genus some qualitatively new sign, namely that the goat in question does not simply have horns but that its horns have some similarity with the horns of the moon.

Psychologically every word formation undergoes three stages of development: (1) the stage of the epithet, (2) the stage of the simile, when the object evokes a new object, (3) the stage of allusion (suggestion, symbolism), when the conflict of the two objects forms a new object not contained in both parts of the simile: the stage of allusion undergoes various phases when a transference of meaning occurs with reference to quantity (synecdoche), quality (metonymy), or when a replacement of the objects themselves occurs (metaphor). In the last case we obtain a *symbol*, i.e. an indivisible unity; the means of depiction in this sense are the means of symbolization, i.e. of the primeval creative act which cannot be further simplified or broken down by knowledge.

The creation of a verbal metaphor (of a symbol, i.e. the joining of two objects into one) is the goal of the creative process; but since this goal is only realized by means of representation, and since the symbol is created, we stand on the border between poetic creation and mythic creation. The independence of the new image 'a' (a perfect metaphor) from the images which gave rise to it ('b', 'c' where 'a' is obtained either in the transference of 'b' to 'c' or, conversely, 'c' to 'b') is expressed by the fact that creation endows it with ontological being, independently of our consciousness; the whole process is reversed: the goal (the metaphor-symbol), having acquired being, is transformed into a real, active cause (the cause of the creation*): the symbol becomes an embodiment. It comes alive and acts indepen-

---

* The power of song, according to Veselovsky,[8] became a common theme in European ballads. 'What is the cause of the singer's song? His song-spell exerts power over the gods.' (A. Veselovsky.) The very process of song-poetic creation is a process of incantation; an incantation creates images; the word creates flesh;

dently: the white horn of the moon becomes the white horn of a mythical being; the symbol becomes a myth; the moon is now the external image of a celestial bull or goat, mysteriously concealed from us: we see the *horn* of this mythical beast though we don't see the beast itself. Every process of artistic creation is, in this sense, mythological, but consciousness is related to 'creative legend' in two ways. Potebnya says: 'Either the image is considered an objective one and thus is wholly transferred in meaning and serves as the basis for further inferences about the properties of the thing signified; or . . . the image is considered only as a subjective means for a transition to meaning and provides no further inferences.'

Mythic creation either precedes aesthetic creation (the conscious use of the means of representation is possible only during the stage of the breaking down of a myth), or follows it (in a period when knowledge is broken down, a period of general scepticism, of cultural decline), reviving in mystical brotherhoods and societies, among people conscious of having lost faith in science, art and philosophy, but still unconsciously carrying with them the living element of creation.

We are experiencing such a period. The religious world-view is alien to us. Philosophy long ago replaced religion, experienced in symbols, with the dogma of metaphysical systems. Science, on the other hand, has destroyed religion. Instead of dogmatic affirmations of God's existence and of the immortality of the soul, science gives us mathematical signs of the relations of phenomena in whose mystical essence we believed just yesterday and cannot believe today when the laws of mechanics which control them are identified.

Poetry is directly bound to the creation of language; and it is

---

the word, having been given flesh in an image, subsequently becomes the apparition of a demon revealed to the song creator. The ancient notion of Apollo as a poetic image turned into a notion of Apollo, the protector of the Muses; he holds a lyre in his hands, given him by Hermes: this is how Veselovsky explains the birth of the legend of Apollo Musagetes.[9]

indirectly bound to mythical creation; the power of the image is directly proportionate to belief (though not conscious belief) in the existence of this image. When I say, 'the moon is a white horn', of course I do not affirm with my consciousness the existence of a mythical animal whose horn I see in the sky in the shape of the moon; but at the deepest level of my creative self-assertion I cannot but believe in the existence of some reality, the symbol or representation of which is the metaphorical image I have created.

Poetic speech is directly bound to mythical creation; the striving for a figurative combination of words is a basic characteristic of poetry.

The real power of creation cannot be measured by consciousness; consciousness always comes after creation; the striving for a combination of words and consequently for the creation of images which emerge out of a new word formation is indicative of the fact that the basis of a creative assertion of life is alive, independent of whether consciousness justifies this striving or not. Such an assertion of the power of creation in words is religious; it exists in spite of consciousness.

And thus the new word of life is nurtured by poetry in a period of general decay. We revel in words because we are conscious of the significance of new, magical words with which, again and again, we are able to cast a spell on the darkness of night which looms above us. We are still alive, but we are alive because we are supported by words.

Play with words is a characteristic of youth; beneath the dust of the fragments of decayed culture we invoke and conjure with the sounds of words. We know that this is the only legacy which will be of use to our children.

Our children will forge the new symbol of belief out of luminous words; the crisis of knowledge will appear to them to be just the death of old words. Mankind is alive as long as the poetry of language exists; the poetry of language is alive.

We are alive.

Notes

1 Fyodr Ivanovich Tyutchev (1803–73), a philosophic poet and militant Slavophile. The line is from the second stanza of his three-stanza poem 'Silentium' (1836): 'How will the heart express itself? / How will another understand you? / Will he understand what it is you live for? / A thought that is spoken is a lie; / by stirring up the springs you will cloud them, / so drink of them, and be silent.'

2 Aleksandr Afanasevich Potebnya (1835–91), a Ukrainian and Russian philologist. His works concern the theory of literature, folklore and ethnology: *Thought and Language* (1862), *Notes on Russian Grammar* (Vols I and II, 1874; Vol. III, 1899); *Notes on the Theory of Literature* (1905).

3 Antoine Fabre d'Olivet (1768–1825), French philosopher and philologist; *La Langue hébraïque restituée* (1815).

4 Aleksandr Nikolaevich Afanasev (1826–71), Russian historian, student of folklore and collector of eight volumes of folktales or *skazki*.

5 Immanuel Kant (1724–1804), the German philosopher. The Russian terms are translations of Kant's 'Zweckmässigkeit ohne Zweck', purposiveness without a purpose, from 'The Critique of Aesthetic Judgement' in *The Critique of Judgement* (1790).

6 Eduard Hanslick (1825–1904), an Austrian music critic and theorist, expressed his aversion to Romantic, emotional aesthetics in *The Beautiful in Music* (1854).

7 In the Russian the use of the instrumental case of *gora* (mountain), *goroyu*, implies identification or likeness with *tucha* (cloud), creating a figurative form somewhat like the hyphenated nouns in English; 'eye-storms' translates the same form.

8 Aleksandr Nikolaevich Veselovsky (1838–1906), a literary historian, writer on comparative folklore and theoretician of the psychology of folklore in *Introduction to Historical Poetics*

(1894) and *The Poetics of Subjects* (1897–1906).
9 Apollo, patron or protector of the Muses.

Aleksandr Blok

Aleksandr Aleksandrovich Blok (1880–1921) was born to a family of liberal intellectuals and brought up by his mother's side. His development as a poet was oriented by extraordinary experiences at the turn of the century, centred upon a female figure of perfection, the Beautiful Lady, and abetted by images and ideas of Vladimir Solovyov. He turned against the latter's Christian context as the focus of his poetry shifted to urban events, the 1905 Revolution and a love affair with the actress N. N. Volokhova (1907). During the War he served in the Pinsk Marshes (1916–17). After the 1917 Revolution, he was busied with official cultural functions and withered in the politicized climate.

WRITINGS

Mostly poetry and lyrical drama. *Poems about the Beautiful Lady* (1904); the play *The Puppet Show* (1906); a collection of poetry, *The Snow Mask* (1907); the play, *The Stranger* (1907); the dramatic poem, *The Song of Fate* (1908); the play, *The Rose and the Cross* (1913); and the long poem, *The Twelve* (1918).

'On the Present State of Russian Symbolism' was first published in the St Petersburg journal *Apollon* in 1910, the revision of a lecture to the Society of the Friends of Eloquence in April 1910, which was given a fortnight after a lecture by Vyacheslav Ivanov entitled 'The Testament of Symbolism'.

ON THE PRESENT STATE OF RUSSIAN SYMBOLISM

The immediate responsibility of the artist is to show and not to prove. In arriving at my response to the lecture by Vyacheslav Ivanovich Ivanov,[1] I must say that I shall avoid speaking of the artist's immediate responsibilities; but the position of Russian literary language today clearly shows that we Russian symbolists have completed a distinct segment of our journey and now face new problems; in such circumstances, when the moment of transition is so clearly defined as it is now, we look for help in memory and, guided by its thread, we ascertain and explain our origins and our native land – more for our own benefit perhaps than for that of others. It is as if we have emerged upon the deck of a ship already far from shore in the immense ocean of life and art; we have not yet sighted another shore which can lure our dreams and our creative will; there are few of us and we are surrounded by enemies; it is high noon and we recognize each other more clearly; cold hands shake one another as the colours of our native land are raised on the mast.

Every artist dreams of 'speaking his soul without words', to borrow Fet's[2] phrase; thus, in order to complete the difficult task I have taken on – to give an account of the path already travelled and to muse on that of the future – I have chosen, for better or worse, a conventional language; and as I agree with the fundamental attitudes of V. Ivanov and also with his method of facilitating the presentation, I shall call my language a language of *illustrations*. My aim is to make concrete what V. Ivanov has said, to lay bare his terminology and paint my illustrations into his text; for I am one of those who does grasp clearly the reality behind his words, which at first glance appears abstract; I ask that my words be considered as words that serve, like the words of a Baedeker which every traveller needs. I dare not say whether one can speak more precisely than I shall; there is, however, no smugness in my words when I tell those who might find my guidebook obscure that the lands I am describing are also obscure. Whoever wishes to understand, will; once I have noted what has taken place and have determined the inner connection of events, my duty will be performed.

Before attempting a description of the thesis and antithesis of Russian symbolism, I must make one more preliminary remark: the history of Russian symbolism is not at issue here; it is impossible to fix an exact chronology of when the events one discusses have taken place and are still taking place in ideal worlds.

The *thesis*: 'you are free in this magic world filled with correspondences'. Create what you like, for *this world belongs to you*. 'Seize, seize all that is secret in us, dusk and daybreak in us' (Bryusov).[3] 'I am the god of a mysterious world, the whole world is in my several dreams' (Sologub).[4] You are the solitary possessor of a treasure; but there are those around you who know of this treasure (or – it only appears that they know, and so it doesn't really matter). Hence – ourselves, the few who know, the symbolists.

From the moment these principles take root in the souls of several people, symbolism begins, a school is formed. This is its first youth, a period of novelty, of first discoveries. Here no one yet knows the other's world, nor does anyone know his own world; people 'wink' at each other and agree that a division exists between this world and ideal 'other worlds'; forces are pooled in the struggle for these yet unknown 'other' worlds.

The daring, inexperienced heart whispers: 'You are free in the magic worlds'; but the edge of the mysterious sword is already placed against the chest. The symbolist is a *theurgist* from the outset, a possessor of secret knowledge, behind which lies a secret activity; but he considers this mystery, which proves only subsequently to be universal, as his own; he sees in it a treasure over which a fern flower blooms at midnight in June, and wishes in the blue of midnight to pluck – the 'blue flower'.

The theurgist dwells in the azure of Someone's radiant

glance; this sword-like glance pierces all worlds; 'waters and rivers, and a distant wood, and peaks of snowy mounts' – and passes through all worlds till it meets him at the beginning – as just a glimmer of Someone's serene smile.

> Whether dozing at noon or waking at night,
>   Someone is there. Two of us –
> Straight into the soul pries her radiant light
>   By day and its darkened lair.
> Ice melts and earnest blizzards quietly end,
>   And flowers unfold anew.
> *But the Name, unique, of the Radiant Friend,*
>   *Has it been given you?*

(V. Solovyov[5])

The worlds which appear to the glance in the light of the radiant sword become more and more enticing; melancholy musical sounds, calls, rumblings, *words* virtually, float up from their depths. At the same time, they begin to *take on a colour* (here one's first profound knowledge of colours begins); finally, that colour, which I find easiest to describe as purple-violet (though this name is perhaps not entirely accurate), predominates.

Piercing the purple of the violet worlds, the golden sword flares up blindingly – and pierces the heart of the theurgist. A face begins to grow visible among the heavenly roses; a voice is discerned, and a dialogue, like that described in Solovyov's *Three Encounters*, begins; the theurgist says: 'Hast Thou not evaded the living gaze three times? Thy face appeared, but I wished to see all of Thee.' The voice says: 'It will come to pass in Egypt.'

This is the end of the thesis. The miracle of solitary transformation begins.

Then, already clearly anticipating the transformation, as though sensing the touch of someone's innumerable hands at his shoulder in the violet-purple twilight which begins to seep into the gold, and foreseeing the approach of some vast funeral, the theurgist answers the calls:

This gold and purple night
We'll go our separate ways,
And I've glimpsed some withdrawn, stormy might
Through heaven's rose in Thy gaze.[6]

The storm's might has already affected the Radiant Countenance, it is *almost* incarnate – that is, *the Name is almost divined*. All has been foreseen except one thing: *the dead centre of the celebration*. This is the most complex moment of the transition from thesis to antithesis which is defined only *a posteriori* and which I am able to recount only by introducing the fiction of someone's outside mediation (the person is unknown to me). The entire pattern of experiences essentially changes, the 'antithesis', the 'transformation', which was already anticipated at the very outset of the thesis, begins. The events which bear witness to this are as follows.

As though jealous of the solitary theurgist's radiant clarity, someone intersects the golden thread of nascent miracles; the blade of the radiant sword grows dim and is no longer felt by the heart. The worlds, which were permeated by its golden light, lose the purple hue; a universal blue-violet twilight bursts forth, as though through a broken dam (Vrubel's[7] work best illustrates all these colours), accompanied by the rending, gypsy-like sounds of fiddles and refrains. If I could paint a picture, I would portray the experiences of this moment like this: a huge, white catafalque swings in the violet twilight of an immense world, and upon it lies a lifeless doll whose face vaguely recalls the one glimpsed amid the heavenly roses.

An extraordinary sharpness and brilliance and variety of experience characterize this moment. All things are fully related in the violet twilight of the worlds crowded together, though the laws of the relations differ completely from those before, since there is no longer a golden sword. Now a joyful sob is heard against the deafening background of an entire wailing orchestra: 'The world is beautiful, the world is magic, you are free.'

Having experienced all this, the theurgist is no longer alone; he is filled with many demons (otherwise called 'doubles'), which the caprice of his evil creative will forms into constantly changing groups of conspirators. With the help of these conspirators he conceals at every moment some part of his soul from himself. Thanks to this network of deceit – the more cunning it is, the more enchanting the surrounding violet twilight – he is able to forge a weapon out of each of the demons, and bind each of the doubles with a pact; they plunder the violet worlds and, obedient to his will, fetch him the most precious things – not one of which he will want: one brings a storm-cloud, another the sigh of the sea, a third amethyst, a fourth a holy scarab, an eye with wings. All this their lord flings into the crucible of *artistic creation*, and finally, with the help of incantation, he obtains the object of the quest – to his own astonishment and amusement; the unknown object of the quest is a pretty doll.

The inevitable has occurred: my own magic world has become the arena of my personal actions, it has become my 'dissecting room' or my *puppet-booth*, where I myself play alongside my amazing dolls (*ecce homo!*). The golden sword has grown dim and the violet worlds have poured into my heart. The ocean is my heart and everything in it is equally enchanted: I do not distinguish the lives, dreams and deaths of this world from those of the other worlds (oh moment, remain!). In other words, I have already made my own life into art (a striking tendency in all European *decadence*). Life became art, I cast a spell and before me arose what I (personally) call the 'stranger': the pretty doll, the deep-blue ghost, the secular miracle.

The antithesis is complete. And I feel a gentle and sublime delight before my creation for quite a while. Violins praise it in their language.

The stranger is not simply a lady in a black dress with ostrich feathers in her hat. She is the diabolic fusion of many worlds, primarily the blue and violet worlds. Had I had the talents of a Vrubel, I would have created a demon; but each performs the task allotted him.

What has been created in such a way – through the spells cast by the artist and the petty demons who serve every artist – has neither beginning nor end, is neither living nor dead.

Splashed with stars, a dress's train,
And a blue, deep blue, blue glance.
Cleaving heaven and earth and heaven again,
A bonfire whirls through a new expanse.

(*The Earth in Snow*)

There, as polar winds howl into the night,
I sought out a ring in the starry field
And lo, amid the lace a face grew bright
A radiant face by the lace concealed,
As trills of her snowy storm shriek by,
Dragging with its train stars all shining,
Like a tambourine whirling on high
With a thousand bells fearfully jangling.

(*Unforeseen Joy*)[8]

This is the creation of art. For me, it is an accomplished fact. I stand before my art's creation and have no idea what I should do: what should I do, in other words, with these worlds, what should I do with my own life which, from that time on, became art, and next to which my creation now *lives* – neither dead nor alive, a dark-blue ghost. I see clearly 'the summer lightning between the brows of clouds' of Bacchus (*Eros* of V. Ivanov), discern clearly the pearly wings (Vrubel's *Demon* and *Tsarevna-Swan*) or hear the rustle of silks ('The Stranger'[9]). But everything is a ghost.

In such circumstances questions arise about the curse of art, about a 'return to life', about 'public service', about the church and 'the people and the intelligentsia'. This is an entirely natural phenomenon, lying of course within the limits of symbolism, since this search for the lost golden sword, which will transfix chaos again, will organize and tame the raging violet worlds.

This searching is valuable since it reveals clearly the *objectivity and reality* of 'those other worlds'; and thus we can positively affirm that all the worlds we have visited and all the events in them are by no means 'our imaginings', that is, 'thesis' and 'antithesis' are far from having one personal meaning. Thus, for example, in the period of this searching, a *Russian revolution* is essentially being evaluated, that is, a revolution is no longer perceived as a *half-reality*, all its partial causes – economic, historical, etc. – are given its highest sanction. To counter-balance the view of a vulgar criticism which says that 'revolution has carried us away', we affirm quite the opposite: the revolution has been completed not only in this but in the other worlds; it was one of the manifestations of the clouding over of the gold and the triumph of the violet twilight, it was, that is, part of those events we have witnessed in our own souls. As something came unstuck in us, the same happened in Russia. The blue ghost that had been created arose before the national soul, just as it had arisen before us. And Russia herself, in the rays of this new civic spirit (by no means Nekrasov's,[10] only by tradition associated with him) proved to be our own soul.

The current state of affairs is like this: the mutiny of the violet worlds is subsiding. The violins, having praised the ghost, reveal their true nature at last: they are able only to sob loudly, to sob when no one wishes to listen; but their loud, triumphant squeal, turning yet again into a sob (this is the sound of the soul of reconciliation which pines in the fields), almost subsides completely. The muffled, melancholy notes can only be heard somewhere beyond the horizon now. The violet twilight vanishes; a barren plain is revealed, it is the soul ravaged by the feast: an empty, remote plain – and above it flies the last warning, a comet. And the bitter smell of almonds is in the rarefied air (a somewhat different version of this is in *my* play, *The Song of Fate*).

The reality I have described is the only one which, for me, gives meaning to life, world and art. Either these worlds exist or they do not. For those who say they do not, we are simply 'middling decadents', fabricators of unprecedented sensations, who write about death only because we ourselves have grown weary.

Speaking personally, I can say that if I ever had the desire to convince anyone of the existence of something beyond and greater than myself, in the end it disappeared; I dare to add, at the same time, that I most humbly ask the honourable critics and public not to waste time misunderstanding my verse, since my verse is only a detailed and consistent description of what I am speaking about in this paper; and I can only refer those who wish to know more about the experiences I have described to my poetry.

If one says yes, that is, if these worlds do exist and everything described could have occurred and has occurred (it is impossible for me not to know this), then it would be strange for us to be seen in any other state than the present one; we are ordered to drink, to enjoy ourselves, to make things alive – but our faces are scorched and disfigured by the violet twilight. A question may be put to those who would call us 'apostles of dream and death' – where were they in the period of thesis and antithesis? Were they not yet born and simply unaware of all of this? Did they or did they not have *these* visions, i.e. are they symbolists or not?

A symbolist can only be born; hence all the external and vulgar obscurantism with which the so-called 'realists' are engrossed, as they try with all their might to become symbolists. These attempts are as transparent as they are pitiful. The sun of naïve realism has set; it is impossible to give a meaning to anything at all outside symbolism. Hence writers, even those with great gifts, can do nothing with art if they are not baptized with the 'fire and spirit' of symbolism. To busy oneself with puzzling fabrications is not yet to be an artist; to be an artist is to weather the wind from the worlds of art, from those thoroughly unlike this world but exerting an awful influence upon it; in these worlds, there is neither cause nor effect, time nor space, carnal nor incorporeal, and these worlds are innumerable: Vrubel saw forty different heads on the Devil, but in fact their number was beyond reckoning.

Art is *Hell*. For good reason V. Bryusov has foreseen the artist's fate thus: 'As with Dante, a subterranean flame must scorch your cheeks.' Only he who has a companion, teacher and guiding vision of That Which leads to where the teacher himself dares not enter may travel the countless circles of Hell and not perish.

What did happen to us in the period of 'antithesis'? What dimmed the golden sword, why did the blue-violet worlds rush in and mingle with this world, creating chaos by making life into art, by sending the blue ghost forth from its depths and by ravaging the soul of the ghost?

This is what: we were 'prophets' and wanted to become 'poets'. In the severe language of my teacher, V. Solovyov, it goes like this:

> The soul's delight for studied device,
> The quick tongue of gods for the patter of a slave,
> The Muses' shrine for a side-show to entice
> Fools – he bartered, he beguiled and misgave.

Yes, all this is true. We entered into beguiling conspiracies with obliging doubles; strengthened with a slavish audacity, we transformed the world into a side-show; we uttered oaths to demons – not to the beautiful ones, only to the pretty ones (and indeed the prettiest of them are slaves – those that are seduced, not those that master), and finally we *beguiled fools*, for 'literary fame' (which is not worth a farthing) visited us notably when we betrayed the 'Muses' shrine', when we came to believe more in the ghost of the antithesis we had created than in the immediate reality of the 'thesis'.

Can what happened to us be repaired or not? At bottom this question begs another: 'Should Russian symbolism exist or not?'

Simple pessimism or simple optimism or just a confession – all this would obscure the question. Our sin (personal and collective) is too great, and so in our present position the solutions are very frightening. In one way or another the violet worlds overwhelmed both Lermontov,[11] who fell voluntarily to the pistol, and Gogol,[12] who burned himself out, floundering in the clutches of a spider; we have experienced before our very eyes something even more expressive: the insanity of Vrubel and the death of Kommissarzhevskaya;[13] it is no accident that events nearly always take this turn with artists – because art is a monstrous and splendid Hell. Diligently the artist traces his images out of the darkness of Hell; thus Leonardo would prepare a black background beforehand so that the features of Devils and Madonnas might stand out; similarly, Rembrandt draws out his dreams from black-red shadows, and Carrière[14] from a grey network of haze. In the same way, Andrei Bely, at the beginning of his brilliant tale (*The Silver Dove*), asks the question: 'And the sky? At first glance its air appeared pale, but then, if scrutinized, did it not look utterly black?. . . . Hey, don't take fright, you're not up in the air. . . .'

But the artist who begins to see other worlds finds himself precisely here, in the black air of Hell. But when the golden sword, extended straight into his heart by someone's Invisible Hand – through all the multicoloured heavens and dense atmospheres of other worlds – dies out, then the worlds mingle, and in the dead midnight of art the artist loses his mind and perishes.

But in the *thesis*, where the presentiment of the twilight of the antithesis is already present, the golden sword is the greatest factor:

I sense Thy coming. Years pass by.
In one form always, I sense Thy coming.

The horizon's all alight, remorseless in clarity.
And in silence I await – pining and loving.
The horizon's all alight, and Thy revelation near.
But terror pricks me: Thou willst change Thy form . . ., etc.
                              (*Verses about the Beautiful Lady*)

We have experienced the madness of the other worlds, having demanded miracles prematurely: the nation's soul met, in fact, the same fate: it asked for miracles too early, and the violet worlds of revolution reduced it to ashes. But something undying exists in the soul – where the soul is a child. In one place in the requiem for children, the deacon ceases to pray for intercession and says simply: 'Thou gavest the *true promise* that *children* shall be *blessed* in Thy Kingdom.'

The true promise was given us in first youth. One must speak about our own and the nation's soul, along with its ashes, in a clear, steadfast voice: 'May it rise from the dead'. Perhaps we ourselves will perish also, but the dawn of that *first* love will remain.

It always seemed as if we had been placed on a lofty mountain from which the kingdoms of the world appeared to us in the unprecedented radiance of a violet sunset; pretty, like queens, but not beautiful, like kings, we devoted ourselves to the sunset and fled the heroic deed. Hence it was so easy for the uninitiated to rush after us; because of this, symbolism became suspect.

We dissolved the 'pearl of love' into the world. But Cleopatra was *Basilis Basileōn* only until that moment when passion compelled her to take the serpent to her bosom.[15] Either destruction in submissiveness or the heroic deed of manliness. The golden sword was given in order to strike.

The heroic deed of manliness must begin with *obedience*. Coming down from the mountain we must become like the prisoner of Reading Gaol:[16]

I never saw a man who looked
  With such a wistful eye

Upon that little tent of blue
　　Which prisoners call the sky,
And at every drifting cloud that went
　　With sails of silver by.

Casting a wistful eye on the little tent of blue, do we find in this empty sky a trace of that gold which once grew dim? Or is our fate that destruction of which artists sometimes fearfully dream? This is destruction from 'playing with chance': it seems that all paths have been searched and all sins atoned for, when, in an unexpected hour, in a lonely street, a leaden brick falls out of an unknown house straight on the head. Lermontov lived by the lyric poetry of chance.

The steed like an arrow his master
From battle to freedom withdrew.
But a bullet flying yet faster
The eased horseman in darkness slew.[17]

This is my conclusion: the path to the heroic deed, which is required if we are to serve, is – foremostly – an apprenticeship, a deepening of the self, a fixing of one's gaze and a spiritual diet. One must learn from the world and from that child which still lives in the burning soul.

The artist must approach daring with timidity, knowing the price of confusing art with life and the value of remaining a simple man. We are bound, in our capacity as artists, to contemplate with clarity all holy conversations (*santa conversatione*) and the overthrow of the Antichrist, like Bellini and Beato. We must remember and hold dear the pilgrimage of Signorelli[18] who, in the autumn of his years, arrived in distant, rocky Orvieto and humbly besought the citizens to allow him to paint the new chapel.

Notes

1 Vyacheslav Ivanovich Ivanov (1866–1949), poet,

philosopher, classical scholar and the leader of the St Petersburg symbolists. The collection of poetry *Eros* appeared in 1907.

2 Afanasy Fet (1820–92), author of short lyric poetry of fine technique.

3 Valery Yakovlevich Bryusov (1873–1924), poet, novelist, playwright and editor of the important symbolist journal *Vesy (The Scales)*. His important volumes of poetry were *Tertia vigilia* (1900) and *Urbi et orbi* (1905), and he wrote a novel, *The Fiery Angel* (1908).

4 Fyodor Sologub was the pseudonym of Fyodr Teternikov (1863–1927), symbolist poet and novelist, and author of the novel *The Petty Demon* (1907).

5 Vladimir Sergeevich Solovyov (1853–1900), philosopher and poet, tried to reconcile Christian doctrine with scientific thought in *The Crisis of Western Philosophy – Against the Positivists* (1874).

6 From Solovyov's autobiographical visionary poem *Three Encounters*.

7 Mikhail Aleksandrovich Vrubel (1856–1910), a Russian painter who died only a week before Blok's lecture. He illustrated Lermontov's narrative poem *The Demon* in 1890, and returned to the subject in 1900 with a series of *Demon* paintings. *Tsarevna–Swan* is from 1900. Vrubel suffered from a mental illness from 1902; in 1906 he lost his sight.

8 *The Earth in Snow* (1908) and *Unforeseen Joy* (1907) are collections of poetry by Blok.

9 A poem by Blok (1906).

10 Nikolai Nekrasov (1821–75) was a poet of the peasantry and the editor of the influential journal *Sovremmenik (The Contemporary)*; after 1856, with the participation of Nikolai Chernyshevsky, it became a militant radical review.

11 Mikhail Lermontov (1814–41), the Russian poet, was exiled in 1840 for duelling, and killed the following year in another duel.

12 Nikolai Gogol (1809–52), Russian-Ukrainian novelist, short-story writer, playwright. He fell under the influence of a fanatical priest, Father Matthew Konstantinovsky, who convinced him he should burn the manuscript of a novel he had been working on for years. Gogol burned the second part of *Dead Souls*, took to bed, refusing all food, and died of starvation.

13 Vera Fyodorovna Kommissarzhevskaya (1864–1910), Russian actress and founder of several theatre companies. She died in February 1910.

14 Eugène Carrière (1849–1906), French painter and lithographer, used an increasingly grey chiaroscuro style which virtually eliminated all colour.

15 Blok's contemporary, the short-story writer A. I. Kuprin, recounts the anecdote about Cleopatra in a tale of 1904, *Diamonds*; according to legend she drank a pearl of a size and a perfection never seen before by dissolving it in vinegar. *Basilis Basileōn* means 'Queen of Queens'.

16 'The Ballad of Reading Gaol' (1898) by Oscar Wilde (1854–1900); the Russian text is by Konstantin Balmont (1867–1943), an early symbolist poet.

17 From Lermontov's poem *The Demon* (1839).

18 Luca Signorelli (1445/50–1523) probably studied with Piero della Francesca. His masterpieces are the frescoes in the chapel of S. Brizio in the Orvieto cathedral, *The End of the World* and *The Last Judgement* (1499–1504).

Index